KAREN McCARTNEY

50/60/70

ICONIC AUSTRALIAN HOUSES
THREE DECADES OF DOMESTIC ARCHITECTURE

PHOTOGRAPHY BY MICHAEL WEE

MURDOCH BOOKS

A WORD FROM PENELOPE SEIDLER AM LFRAIA

The houses that feature in the following pages, as selected by Karen McCartney, represent the grand variety that flourished in Australian post-World War II architecture. It is heartening that the first edition of the book was treasured by so many to warrant the demand for another printing, bringing it to a wider audience.

For the most part, the houses here are simple family homes, with timeless design integrity, happily lacking the pretension and pseudo stylistic features that characterise much contemporary design. They are each a time capsule of their era. They also have a connection, in one way or another, with the landscape. Perhaps more than anything else, this is what identifies that period. With the end of the war came the breaking down of many boundaries and an awareness and engagement with the outdoors: you'll see many large glass areas, blurring the edges between inside and out, along with large balconies for outdoor living. Interiors were opened up, with space flowing between the interior and exterior, as well as between rooms, rather than the boxed rooms and corridors that were present in earlier architecture. Of the fifteen architects included in the book, all are males, and four are immigrants who were educated overseas. All of the houses, however, are Australian.

It is unfortunate that many houses of the era have been demolished or grossly altered, only to be replaced by overbearing mansions with fake columns and arches and no design integrity. It is to be hoped that with the community's increasing awareness of the *Copyright Amendment (Moral Rights) Act* of December 2000, any owners wishing to 'upgrade' their property will need to do so in consultation with the original architect or their estate, thereby maintaining the architectural integrity.

Harry Seidler, writing in the *Bulletin* in October 1989, said of the Australian style that it is the successful response to the climate and our informal way of life, rather than an identifiable 'style'. Nowhere is this better illustrated than in the diverse range of houses depicted in this book. Karen McCartney is to be congratulated for gathering these houses together in this beautiful book, sharing the enjoyment that they bring with a wider audience and preserving them in these pages.

CONTENTS

INTRODUCTION

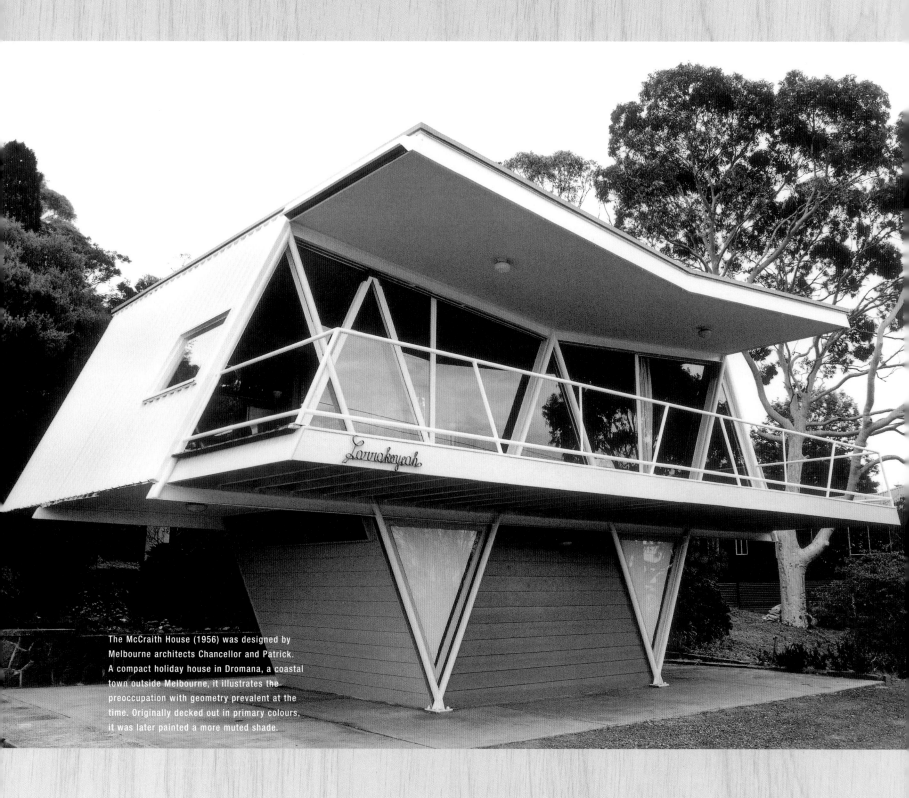

The McCraith House (1956) was designed by
Melbourne architects Chancellor and Patrick.
A compact holiday house in Dromana, a coastal
town outside Melbourne, it illustrates the
preoccupation with geometry prevalent at the
time. Originally decked out in primary colours,
it was later painted a more muted shade.

MANY OF TODAY'S NEW HOUSES ARE DESIGNED with a level of indulgence and luxurious use of space that could not have been imagined 60 years ago. Media rooms, multiple bathrooms with spa-style fittings, music rooms, in-house gymnasiums and swimming pools were once the territory of the rich industrialist rather than someone in middle management. Hence it is hard from this position of prosperity to conceive of the level of limitation Australians experienced in the postwar years. Nothing was thrown away nor taken for granted. Clothes were handed down, furniture was fixed, food continued to be rationed – the 'mend and make-do' mentality pervaded every aspect of life.

The war years (1939–45) were particularly grim for the architectural profession, and many small firms closed through lack of work. Materials were scarce and domestic buildings were subject to strict guidelines in terms of expenditure and size. The maximum floor space allowed was 14 squares (135 m^2) and an *Australian Home Beautiful* editorial in 1942 pointed to maximum costs of £3000 for a new house and a ceiling of £250 on renovations. These restrictions continued in the postwar years and, because of the desperate need for housing with the wave of new migrants and the numbers of returned servicemen, the drive was often for quantity over quality. Aesthetics tended to give way to economics as the state controlled the entire process; the architects, engineers, designers and town planners all fell under one great bureaucratic umbrella.

An estimated 400,000 homes were needed, and to solve the housing crisis, the government looked both to local and overseas companies for quick-to-assemble housing. The Commonwealth Government (in conjunction with private enterprise) undertook a fact-finding mission to Europe to source the most suitable housing options, and subsequently bought prefab housing from Sweden and Great Britain. In his book *Australian Architecture 1901–51, Sources of Modernism*, Donald Leslie Johnson notes that 'probably the largest order for English prefabs came from the Australian government when it purchased a batch of factory made timber dwellings called the Riley-Newsum house as late as 1951: cost of 1,250,000 pounds sterling. Made in Lincoln and shipped to Australia in a series of panels.'

Set out in neat quarter acre suburban blocks, these houses had few of the refinements of previous decades, as Jennifer Taylor describes in her essay 'Beyond the 1950s': 'The design features that had made the bungalow such a suitable building type for the 1930s and 1940s could no longer be achieved under the restrictions. "Luxuries" such as eaves, porches, verandas and fireplaces disappeared. In its stripped down form the Australian house had few redeeming qualities.'

The arrangement of rooms also reflected a bygone era. The living room and master bedroom faced the street and corridors led to a separate kitchen and dining room, while the rear of the building housed the bathroom and laundry with access to the yard. Basically, the plan consisted of boxy rooms with little thought given to either the relationship between them, or to the link between indoor and outdoor space. Orientation was a given – the house faced the street regardless of sun or site.

While this was true of the broad sweep of development, there were exceptions. It was a time where young architects felt a sense of opportunity to build a better world and there were ingenious plans by some, working within the restrictions, to maximise the sense of space by losing wasteful corridors and opening up kitchen and dining rooms to one larger area. Notable is the Beaufort House, designed by Arthur Baldwinson in conjunction with the Beaufort Division of the Department of Aircraft Production, which was shown in prototype to the public in 1946. Using technology developed for aircraft manufacture, this steel-framed house was an innovative attempt to contribute to solving the housing problem. The Vandyke Brothers in Sydney also provided local product with, amongst more traditional designs, the Sectionist house, created in 1946.

'Australia is the small house. Ownership of one in a fenced allotment is as inevitable and unquestionable a goal of the average Australian as marriage,' wrote architect and architectural critic Robin Boyd in the preface to his 1952 book, *Australia's Home*.

He also noted that 'it was said that flats were for foreigners.' And, indeed, Australia was becoming home to many émigrés. From 1947, Australia was open to British residents but, despite considerable uptake, it was recognised that without further substantial immigration, the country would not flourish. Agreements were made with Malta in 1948 and Italy in 1951, followed by Greece in 1952 and Hungary in 1956. It is estimated that by the end of 1956, more than 1.5 million immigrants had arrived on Australian shores, all within the confines of the White Australia Policy. Promotional material targeting houseproud immigrants showed photographs of an immaculately maintained suburban bungalow and garden with the caption,

'Australians…like to take refreshments out of doors and cultivate neat gardens.'

THE SPIRIT OF THE FIFTIES

The arrival of the Fifties, with its increasing economic prosperity, brought a breezy optimism and a strong consumer drive. Putting the hardship of the war years well behind them, Australians wanted the latest in mod cons, fridges, cars and a new style of home that reflected the spirit of the times. Magazines such as *Australian Home Beautiful* and *House & Garden* drove trends and influenced opinion.

It was the beginning of the marketing of a 'lifestyle'. For a society that had made do, the desire for this new, shiny, ordered suburban life was irresistible. It is therefore understandable that the state-of the-art kitchen at the Rose Seidler House, with its cutting-edge appliances, caused as much excitement as the radical building itself. Advertisements in magazines illustrated Cary Grant and Grace Kelly look-alikes, with two perfect children, perusing plans and a model for their new house built in Hardie's Fibrolite under the heading 'Don't Dream…Build'. *The Age* RVIA Small Homes Service in Melbourne, launched in 1947, with Robin Boyd as director, showcased a range of 40 architect-designed plans for new homes which could be bought for £5. Public uptake was such that by 1951, they were providing plans for 10 percent of all new housing in Victoria. From 1957, plans were also available at the Home Plan Service Bureau at the Myer Emporium, Melbourne, and in 1962, Lend Lease's Carlingford Homes Fair in Sydney proved popular to the tune of two million visitors eager to see the latest in architect-designed project homes. Standard house

plans were even published alongside knitting patterns in *The Australian Women's Weekly*. Clearly, the public had taken Hardie's call to action in their Fibrolite advertisement to heart. Australians were no longer dreaming…they were building.

A NEW APPROACH

Postwar was a period of staggering creativity and originality in Melbourne. There was a spirit of invention in the air as new ideas were generated, new materials and technologies explored and individuality celebrated. A handful of architects worked with site and client to realise exuberant schemes and one-off solutions.

Roy Grounds, who had enjoyed a very successful career before the war, championed a geometric approach to architecture. On the other hand, younger architects experimented with shape and materials in daring ways – Peter McIntyre, for instance, built his own house, a radical A-frame steel structure, with infill panels of Stramit, a compacted straw sheet material. Necessity is the mother of invention and a shortage of materials saw the introduction of lightweight steel frames and, as in Kevin Borland's Rice House, a series of thin concrete-sprayed shells. Cantilevered balconies and window walls; cable supports and plywood ceilings; colour and form; playfulness and theatre – the confidence of experimentation knew no bounds.

A newly found affluence resulted in an increased interest in the holiday house. At one end of the spectrum was the commission from extremely cultured clients John and Sunday Reed for architects McGlashan and Everist to design a house right on the sand at Aspendale, a suburb outside Melbourne. At the opposite end of

A corner of Bruce Robertson's first house
for his family in Sydney's Seaforth (1953).
The opening ply panels increased ventilation
in this west-facing area of the home.

The interior of a Sydney Ancher house in Sydney's lower North Shore suburb of Neutral Bay (1957) shows open-plan living to a degree that was considered revolutionary. The treatment of the ceiling adds a graphic quality to the space.

Brisbane architecture firm Hayes and Scott designed the Harvey Graham Beach House in 1953 with its notable geometric murals. International journals were a great influence on Australian architects and the Case Study Houses of Charles Eames and Eero Saarinen could well have been a source of inspiration for this mural.

the scale, advertisements incorporating plans appealed to home builders to buy sheeting material and construct simple beach shacks themselves.

Another prominent architect designing beach houses (as well as country properties and city residences) in the Fifties for wealthy Melbourne clients was gentleman architect Guilford Bell. He trained in London in the 1930s where he worked on a house restoration project for author Agatha Christie. His 1952 design for Sir Reginald Ansett's Hayman Island resort exposed Bell's refined aesthetic to a range of potential clients. Working mainly as a sole practitioner (he had a brief partnership with Neil Clerehan in 1961 and

later, until Bell's death, with Graham Fisher) on domestic residences, his signature modern elegance found full expression in the Fairfax Pavilion (1969) designed for art collector James Fairfax in Bowral, NSW, and the Seccull House (1972), in Brighton, Victoria. In both, the excellent working relationship with the clients encouraged a freedom of expression, resulting in exceptional examples of Bell's work.

Melbourne's virtuoso performance was, however, short-lived. As Peter McIntyre admitted, it is hard to make a living out of radical thinking but, for this period, Melbourne was, as Robin Boyd said, Australia's 'cradle of modernity'.

TESTING POPULAR TASTE

In Sydney an early and influential pioneer of modernism was Sydney Ancher. He had spent several years in Europe in the early-to-mid Thirties and returned to Australia filled with enthusiasm for the work of Ludwig Mies van der Rohe. 'In designing my houses, I think I have Mies at the back of my mind,' he said. In 1937 he designed what is now considered one of Sydney's most important prewar buildings, the Prevost House, for his architectural partner Reginald Prevost and family. His career went into a holding pattern when he went to war but, upon his return in 1945, he took up where he had left off, designing domestic buildings in the

Neil Clerehan's house for his family (1957)
in Fawkner Street, South Yarra, Melbourne, shows
the use of Stegbar's window wall to full effect.

'I WAS A MAD MODERNIST FROM 1934, HARD LINE AND HARD CORE, MY MOTHER GAVE ME A SUBSCRIPTION TO *AUSTRALIAN HOME BEAUTIFUL*, AND I WOULD TAKE PUBLIC TRANSPORT AROUND MELBOURNE SPOTTING THE MODERNIST HOUSES THAT I LIKED.

Ten years later I met Robin Boyd who was my sergeant in the army (he was an extraordinary influence on me) and when I told him of all the houses I had admired, it turned out they were all designed by the one firm – Grounds and Mewton. We were very envious of Americans at the end of the war. Because of the building boom, there were lots of opportunities to design contemporary houses. I admired the work of Neutra and Ellwood although both were slightly stand-offish in person. There were all sorts of difficulties obtaining materials in Australia. Getting plain, coloured laminate was like getting a drink in the Prohibition, and the 'cream Australia policy' was in full swing – you just couldn't get white appliances. I did make the pilgrimage to Sydney to see the Rose Seidler House when it was finished. It did amaze me, but seemed somehow unrelated to Australia. I was impressed with all the Eames and Saarinen furniture he was able to get from the USA.
I took over from Boyd in 1954 as Director of *The Age* Small Homes Service [Clerehan is at present the newspaper's longest standing contributor], which provided plans to young couples who couldn't afford custom-built but wanted a modern housing solution. During that time I encountered a tremendous range of people. There was a wave of immigration and sign language became very useful!
The training and discipline of thinking small was of great use to me when I designed a project house of 10 squares [93m²] for Pettit and Sevitt called the 3130 house which was a great success both in Victoria and NSW.
The so-called "Nuts and Berries" school in Sydney did have an effect on me – it softened me – but these days I am back to white precision. It allows people and furniture to stand out in a room.'
MELBOURNE ARCHITECT NEIL CLEREHAN

International Style. Ancher's experiences with local councils are significant in that they reveal something of the prevailing attitudes towards the new thinking in architecture. The 1945 design for his own house, Poyntzfield, in Killara, Sydney, was only approved by council after he altered the original plan for a steel-framed building to a more traditional brick construction with a pitched roof. It still won the Sulman Medal in 1946.

The second battle with council in 1946 was more serious, and groundbreaking in its outcome. Ancher designed a house for Mervyn Farley on a magnificent headland site at North Curl Curl. It was a small open-plan house with an extensive terrace (external space was not counted in the size restrictions and so it made sense to exploit it as much as possible) and elegant cantilevered concrete roof extending 1.5m beyond the walls. Warringah Council objected, but agreed to pass the design if a parapet 600mm high were put in place to disguise the flat roof which was considered an 'affront to decency'. The case went to the Land and Valuation Court of NSW. Speaking for the appeal was eminent architect and writer Walter Bunning, while W.R Roach, Chief Health and Building Inspector for Warringah Shire, spoke against it. Roach commented that the building was 'not pleasant, too stark and very different. More like a gun emplacement on North Head than a house.' Despite the reactionary views, the appeal was upheld, the flat roof was vindicated and Australia could join the rest of the world in adopting this signature feature of the modern movement. It did not inhibit councils continuing to object on aesthetic grounds. Harry Seidler, no stranger to the courts, once remarked that he was tired of having to prove his houses innocent.

INTERNATIONAL STYLE VS ORGANIC ARCHITECTURE

In Sydney in 1950 Harry Seidler, who had trained at Harvard Graduate School under Walter Gropius and Marcel Breuer, had completed his modernist masterpiece in the International Style: the Rose Seidler House. Ancher's interpretation of International Style was tempered to a degree to suit local conditions and tastes; the Rose Seidler House, in contrast, was in absolute adherence to its principles – so much so that the house has been described by architectural writer Elizabeth Farrelly as 'built manifesto'.

While Ancher and Seidler were exponents of the International Style, there was another mood afoot in architecture which drew its inspiration from the work of American architect Frank Lloyd Wright (1867–1959), whose Fallingwater (1935) is one of the world's most famous domestic buildings. Certain core principles carried throughout Wright's long career. The relationship of the building to its site was of paramount importance and his houses tended to be low, horizontal structures in natural materials – wood, stone, timber and concrete – which were left unadorned. The influence of his Usonian houses, designed from 1936, can be seen in the work of Peter Muller, Neville Gruzman and Bruce Rickard, the latter commenting on the houses' 'scale, the use of space, the warmth and mellow look from natural materials'. These architects, in particular, identified strongly with Wrightian principles, which they adopted freely and adapted to suit their own aesthetic, the needs of the client and the site. Each house was seen as an individual exercise, whereas the International Style aimed for a superlative design that could provide a solution to any site, anywhere.

In his book *Australia's Home*, Robin Boyd compares these two schools of thought and practice, and expresses with clarity what they hold in common.

'However, the two schools shared many more fundamental precepts. In breaking with the popular stylistic conventions of the day, both believed that they were restoring the dignity of architecture. Both believed simplicity to be the omnipotent law of all design. Both rejected the idea of composing the façades of a building to preconceived rules. Both accepted spatial composition as the expressive field of architecture. Both believed that the building's function was the only basis for planning and that it should (and would automatically if permitted) be expressed in the building's form. Both believed that no material should be twisted into unnatural forms or asked to perform an unsuitable task.'

Despite these philosophical similarities, the resulting buildings could not have been more different. Seidler pulled no punches. 'Does not this [organic] architecture seem rather weak, subservient and not very proud of itself?' he said. Battle lines were drawn, particularly in Sydney, with architects such as Neville Gruzman rising repeatedly to the debate.

In a recent e-mail exchange with Peter Muller, I asked him if he was aware of Seidler's quote at the time. Although he did not recall it, it didn't surprise him, and he clarified his view on the matter. 'Seidler was pushing for International architecture which abnegated all concerns to preserve local diversity. The climatic, the geographic, cultural and spiritual integrity, and deeper

meanings for ornament were regarded as some kind of superstition. So-called organic architecture was regarded as "romantic" and intuitive, rather than intelligent and no match for what the Brave New World had to offer with its high-tech, machine-driven materials. Today, of course, with concerns for global warming, fossil fuels and so on, emphasis shifts once again and the use of natural and sustainable materials in an intelligent and sensible way to reduce energy overloads is considered admirable and strong minded. Pride comes before a fall, subservience to Truth is a blessing and the weak shall inherit the earth.'

Beginning in the early Fifties there was a developing movement in Sydney (a collection of individual architects but sometimes called a 'school' because of like-minded attributes) towards houses that embraced the Wrightian principles. These were often built on steep, difficult-to-access sites which were, as a result, relatively cheap to buy. They were located predominantly in bushland settings on Sydney's North Shore, often battleaxe blocks not visible from the street. In *An Australian Identity: Houses for Sydney 1953–63*, Jennifer Taylor makes the point that there was a conscious 'denial of pretentious display' and an 'intentional understatement'. The relationship to the land was central and the desire to integrate the building with the site with as little disruption as possible was the architect's goal. In 1955, Peter Muller built a house for himself at Whale Beach which accommodated the existing trees and rocks, and his palette of building materials reflected the colours of the landscape, blending one with the other.

Muller claimed he was 'not much of a functionalist...a plan that just works isn't architecture'. These were often the homes of creative people – writers, artists, potters and architects themselves. In an era where the English country garden was still popular, it was considered somewhat 'alternative' to appreciate the native plants and bushland settings. The house Russell Jack designed on the upper North Shore for artist Tony Tuckson and his wife, Margaret, is invisible from the street and entirely open on one side to the bushland. Margaret Tuckson has lived there for nearly 50 years surrounded by art and ceramics.

Taking the bush setting to the ultimate of integration is the Glass House by Ruth and Bill Lucas, in Sydney's Castlecrag. Designed in 1957, this glass pavilion illustrates the idea of 'barely there' structures and shows how Bill Lucas felt the frame was of crucial importance and 'everything that goes on after that destroys the original structure'. Built for his family, and constructed with economy in mind, the house utilises standardised sections of steel, timber and glass.

OUTSIDE INFLUENCES

Travel was crucial for this generation of architects. Often their architectural degrees were practical in nature, covering carpentry, building techniques, engineering and classical architecture, but with little emphasis on contemporary buildings and current ideas. Exposure to other cultures and significant buildings in Europe and the United States was enormously influential. As, indeed, were the architectural journals of the day. George Henderson, who worked for 'regional modernists' Hayes

'I JOINED THE NSW GOVERNMENT ARCHITECT'S OFFICE AS A STUDENT TRAINEE ON A SCHOLARSHIP AT THE AGE OF 16.

Harry Rembert, the Assistant Government Architect, was my mentor and a good designer himself. He took great pleasure in creating a design studio, which hadn't existed before. The Public Works Department had been rather dormant, but accelerated during my time there. When I started, there were six people in the studio, and by the time I left in 1964 there were 25. In 1958, Michael Dysart and I entered the Taubman's Family Home Competition through the *Women's Weekly*. We won £2000, which was quite a large sum then. The calls started coming in from people who wanted a house design – something cheap – and this started me thinking about the whole process of economy. We were asked to design houses for exhibitions – first for Cherrybrook Estate, and then in 1961 we were approached to design three houses for the Lend Lease Carlingford exhibition. Essentially these were exhibitions of architect-designed houses, with all the well-known names there. Lend Lease and Sunline Homes were the two players in the project homes market, and then Sunline Homes collapsed financially. Out of the collapse came Brian Pettit and Ron Sevitt's partnership. Pettit & Sevitt differentiated itself by being absolutely modern with no compromise towards the more conservative mindset. By 1963, they were selling upwards of 200 houses per year.

The launch of Pettit & Sevitt was concurrent with the design of my own house, the Mosman House, which explored my strong attraction to directness of detail and natural materials without artifice. I believe in building in a pragmatic way where the architecture is a result of making selections, judgements and choices. If you are sensible, you see the potential outcome of those choices as higher than the components. Then you have the chance of achieving something artistic. You have earned the right to be an artist because the practicalities have been covered.'

SYDNEY ARCHITECT KEN WOOLLEY

Ken Woolley's Mosman House (1962), looking towards the dining area on the top level and the living area on the lower level – all unified under one sloping roof line.

Ken Woolley's drawing of the celebrated Mosman House.

Photographs taken during the construction of the Fombertaux House (completed 1966) in Sydney's Lindfield East, show the precarious nature of the frame construction. While the house has a precision exterior, the interior allowed nature to intrude: a large rock forms part of the wall in the study.

and Scott, in Brisbane, and later for Seidler, recalls the subscriber copies of international magazines coming into the office. Pages were torn out and filed under the various architects of interest: Alvar Aalto, Marcel Breuer, Eero Saarinen, Charles Eames, Mies van der Rohe and so on, each with their own file to be pored over and absorbed. Also significant was the role of émigrés as teachers and architects. Hayes and Scott. for example, were influenced by Dr Karl Langer, from Vienna, whose 1944 booklet, *Sub-tropical Housing,* advocated, amongst other things, long, shallow floor plans which allowed maximum penetration of natural light. Langer also developed the first sun chart

for Brisbane, a copy of which every architectural practice had, and which was continually used at Hayes and Scott in their quest for optimum orientation.

Architects themselves brought a European sensibility to Australia. 1957, for instance, was the year that Danish architect Jørn Utzon's design for the Sydney Opera House was picked, the story goes, from a pile of rejected entries by the great American architect Eero Saarinen, who missed the early stages of the judging. Amongst local architects, Seidler's philosophy was shaped by the direct teachings of Gropius and Breuer; Taglietti came from postwar Italy where he was taught by Carlo Mollino and Pier Luigi

Nervi; Iwanoff came from Bulgaria, and Buhrich from Germany via Holland and London. The influence of these architects on the local architectural landscape varies depending on their ability to practise. Seidler had no difficulties registering with the Board of Architects, perhaps because his qualifications were from the USA. Taglietti was permitted to practise through the Department of the Interior in Canberra, but both Iwanoff and Buhrich had a long battle with the Board before they were allowed to register and this had a limiting effect on their careers.

Architects who did travel were often able to find an inspirational source that resonated strongly with their natural

This architectural office (1958) of Robertson & Hindmarsh was built on the land of the family house in Sydney's Seaforth. (When the office moved it became a hangout for the teenage children.) Copper panels clad an oregon frame, and the glass wall faced the view over the water. While it made a dramatic architectural statement in close-up, from a distance it melded into the surrounding bushland.

inclination. For Bruce Rickard, who went to the USA in the Fifties, it was Wright's Usonian houses, while for Neville Gruzman, some of whose houses were inspired by Wright, the major influence was Japanese architecture. He was not alone. Le Corbusier and Gropius had already earmarked the Katsura Imperial Villa in Kyoto as praiseworthy for its use of modular space, simplicity and absence of extraneous detailing. Many attributes of Japanese architecture have been adopted for use in Australian domestic architecture: the tradition for post and beam construction; extensive use of wood and the exposure of the structural elements; sliding screens for flexible floor plans; changes in internal levels; framed garden views and the linking of internal and external space. Throughout this book the influence of Japanese architecture can be seen, particularly in the work of Gruzman, Boyd, Jack, McGlashan and Everist and McKay.

The houses shown in this book illustrate the diversity that occurred during the late Sixties and early Seventies. In Perth, Iwanoff had made concrete block his material of choice and his decorative façades became his signature. External patterning was matched by elaborate internal room dividers and bar areas with sculptural cutaway shapes. In Sydney both Collins and Buhrich were influenced by boat building in fibreglass. Collins constructed a whole house in the material while Buhrich's fire-engine red moulded fibreglass bathroom is a high-design statement in a house with no shortage of individual ideas. Kenny, in Melbourne, had an early training under Kevin Borland, a socialist thinker, and his house was designed in modules in the hope that the concept would be adopted by a forward-thinking project home manufacturer. Unfortunately, that was not to be.

McKay's holiday house for photographer David Moore is, on the other hand, a one-off. Spare, utilitarian, and integrated into its rocky site, it is a design that is so site-specific it could never be repeated.

Stan Symonds' house for John and Margaret Schuchard (1963) in Sydney's Seaforth is possibly the best known work of this architect for whom the term 'organic futurist' is a fitting description.

'THERE IS AN INCIDENT THAT I ALMOST FEEL DEFINES MY CAREER. I WAS AT A DRINKS PARTY AND A FELLOW ARCHITECT CAME UP AND INTRODUCED HIMSELF.

"I am Harry Howard. Who are you?" he asked. I said that I was Stan Symonds. "Don't give me that bullshit, we all know that Stan Symonds is a name made up by a group of architects who want to do way-out work and not be identified."
My work was acknowledged early on in my career with *The Australian Journal of Architecture and Arts* devoting a single issue to my projects in 1963. It included already built houses with proposals for apartment blocks. By that time, I had completed the Walsh House at Sackville on the flood-prone Hawkesbury River (1959), and an appreciation was growing for my shell-concrete work. The Jobson House at Bayview (1960), dubbed "The Egg and I" by the neighbours, was designed for Carl Jobson and his wife, Irene, who was a sculptor and potter and appreciated the form of the house. The Schuchard House (1963) at Seaforth was something of an owner-builder project. You see, concrete was as cheap as chips and form work wasn't expensive. Concrete is my material of choice because of its plasticity. You can mould it to any shape, precast it, cast it on site, hand mix or machine mix. The result is highly sculptural architecture. My houses are very much site-specific. I spend time wandering around experiencing the site, the context, the view. The design is the combination of first thoughts and the experience of being there. It has to look like it belongs. I have always worked that way and continue to do so.'

SYDNEY ARCHITECT STAN SYMONDS

The Seccull House (1972) in Melbourne's Brighton was one of Guilford Bell's most satisfying houses. The relationship with the client was so good that the project became a wonderful example of Bell's restrained and elegant approach to domestic architecture.

THE LEGACY

From the Fifties onwards, the kitchen slowly infiltrated the dining and living space – perhaps echoing women's literal and metaphorical move from the confines of the walled-in kitchen. The kitchens themselves, often surprisingly small, modest yet ingeniously fitted out, were tucked behind partial walls or banks of storage cabinets, as in the Buhrich House. The open-plan kitchen/living/dining room (with direct access to a courtyard or 'outdoor room') that every house renovation aspires to today can find its antecedents in the relaxing of divisions, and the linking of spaces, pioneered by the forward-thinking architects featured on these pages.

Few of the architects (except perhaps Neville Gruzman and Guilford Bell, who both had a penchant for the glamorous effect of multiple mirrors) prefigured the rise of the bathroom as such an important room, or rooms, in the house. Of all the houses I visited, Buhrich's red bathroom is a stand-out concept, and Kenny's sliding doors onto a courtyard give an added dimension. The rest are small, functional places to wash and go.

What has altered drastically is the scale of homes. While the postwar restriction of 134 m^2 was undeniably small, the average new house is now 264 m^2 with 600 m^2 not unheard-of. In some cases, with children leaving home later, they have to house two generations of adults, accommodate areas of privacy and provide space for the enormous amount of material goods we all acquire. Designwise, few domestic buildings, in this present look-at-me culture, share the Sydney School's desire for modesty and lack of pretension. As Neil Clerehan pointed out, 'We never imagined there would be a trend for Neo-Historicism. We thought we were forging a brand new way forward.' Indeed, while visiting Russell Jack in Sydney's Wahroonga, I parked opposite his rather hard-to-locate house, beside two enormous house developments, complete with columns and portico, pitched roofs and small windows.

This steel-framed house by Glenn Murcutt in Sydney's Terrey Hills (1972–73) is a Miesian box-like structure in its bushland setting. Murcutt visited the site after a bushfire, when blackened trees formed the landscape, and subsequently chose to clad the house's exterior in black tiles. The house shows the beginnings of Murcutt's interest in connecting the house with its setting.

There is much to be learnt from looking back and, hopefully, the examples contained in this book, and many others like them, will be around to inspire and inform new generations of architects. Sadly, as Professor Philip Goad pointed out, many of the light-structured Fifties buildings on valuable sites have already been demolished.

I came across this quote in *Untold Stories* by Alan Bennett, describing the demolition of his alma mater, Leeds Modern School. It reminds him of what Brendan Gill, a writer for *The New Yorker*, called the 'Gordon Curve' after architect Douglas Gordon of Baltimore.

'This posits that building is at its maximum moment of approbation when it is brand new, that it goes steadily downhill and at 70 reaches its nadir. If you can get a building past that sticky moment, then the curve begins to go up again very rapidly until at 100 it is back where it was in year one. A 100-year-old building is much more likely to be saved than a 70-year-old one.'

Many of these houses are in middle-age and have a long way to go to three score and ten. Let's hope, with the help of sympathetic owners and bodies such as the Historic Houses Trust, Docomomo and the Robin Boyd Foundation, they make it to their centenary.

AT A TIME WHEN AUSTRALIA WAS STRUGGLING TO FIND A NATIONAL ARCHITECTURAL STYLE, ALONG CAME THIS BRASH YOUNG MAN WITH AMERICAN TRAINING AND A EUROPEAN SENSIBILITY, WHO BUILT A RELENTLESSLY MODERN HOUSE IN THE INTERNATIONAL STYLE IN THE HEART OF SUBURBAN BUSHLAND.

PREVIOUS PAGES: Set amongst the bushland of a conservative northern Sydney suburb is the house architect Harry Seidler designed for his parents. A passionate exponent of the International Style, Seidler exploited the principles he had learnt training under architectural greats Walter Gropius and Marcel Breuer. OPPOSITE: The exterior mural was designed and painted by Seidler himself. The colours are repeated in the interior to link the two spaces – blue in the curtains, yellow in the kitchen and grey in the paint colours of the walls.

THE HOUSE THAT HARRY SEIDLER DESIGNED and built for his parents in Wahroonga, on Sydney's North Shore, was completed in 1950. It launched his career, defined the decade and caused a considerable stir. Not only did it excite the architectural establishment but it also attracted public interest in a way that domestic architecture rarely did. Visiting the perfectly preserved house more than 50 years later, it still feels daringly modern, so it's easy to imagine the curious public who came all those years ago to gawp at the house that Harry built.

Harry Seidler was born in 1923 in Vienna, where he lived with his well-to-do parents, Max and Rose, in an apartment remodelled by avant-garde architect Fritz Reichl. With the Nazi occupation of Austria in 1938, Seidler followed his brother Marcell to England, and was taken as a refugee to live with two English ladies in Cambridge, where he attended school for 18 months after which he was interned, first in Liverpool, then the Isle of Man, before being transported to Canada. After his release in 1941, he gained a first class honours degree from the University of Manitoba before winning a scholarship to Harvard Graduate Design School.

The period at Harvard was to be a defining experience for him. Walter Gropius, founder of the Bauhaus movement, and Marcel Breuer, a teacher and practitioner of the Bauhaus principles of design, ran the postgraduate course. Later, Seidler worked as Breuer's chief assistant in his architectural practice in New York, studied design with Josef Albers (a former Bauhaus teacher) in the short-lived, but highly influential Black Mountain College, North Carolina, and spent a summer with flamboyant modernist Oscar Niemeyer in Brazil. All combined to ensure that by the time Seidler moved to Australia, at the behest of his parents, he had experienced an amazing exposure to the world's most influential architects and teachers. At 25, his architectural mindset was confident, complete and ready to be exercised.

'Rose Seidler House may look like a young architect's house for his parents but really it is built manifesto, representing all the Modernist principles of Australia's most famous modern architect...As an attention getter the house remains unbeaten. A homage to Seidler's former New York employer Marcel Breuer, this house – with its TV-screen frontality, open pinwheel plan and elevated trapdoor entry – perches on the grassy site like an arrival from space.' This remarkably astute quote from Elizabeth Farrelly's article in *The Sydney Morning Herald* in 2005 sums up the house as a statement of intent.

At a time when Australia was struggling to find a national architectural style, along came this brash young man with American training and a European sensibility, who built a relentlessly modern house in the International Style in the heart of suburban bushland.

While the design came about with apparent ease, the construction was fraught with difficulty. There were problems finding a builder to undertake such a radical project, but with the help of well-established architect Sydney Ancher, Seidler appointed Bret Lake. In the postwar period, materials were not easy to come by and there are stories of Seidler driving around building sites picking up a few bricks here, a few bricks there.

Even the siting of the house was considered unusual. In an era where the

The cantilevered cabinet, which spans the rear wall of the living space, was made by Paul Kafka, a fellow immigrant from Vienna. The mix of timber, finished in matt black paint, and the reflective qualities of black glass is highly effective. Just visible in the reflection are the Grasshopper chairs by Eero Saarinen and the Calder-style mural.

THIS PAGE: The fireplace, in rough hewn sandstone, is one of the few areas where the natural and haphazard intrudes into this precision interior. It also acts as a divider between the living and dining areas. OPPOSITE: The dining table, made by Paul Kafka, is surrounded by plywood DCM chairs, designed in 1946 by Charles and Ray Eames. Between the dining area and kitchen is a sliding section of opaque glass to provide access to one from the other.

ABOVE: Looking along the cabinet to the bright orange wall of curtaining.
OPPOSITE: This outdoor area is accessed via the ramp or directly from the living area. The colours and shapes in the mural are echoed in the choice of the famous Butterfly chair, the curvaceous form and solid-coloured canvas covers of which couldn't be more apt. All the furnishing in the house is as originally specified and shows the architect's ability to think in terms not only of the structure but also of the aesthetics of the interior.

front door inevitably faced the street, the Rose Seidler House is positioned in the centre of the block, with trees providing privacy and floor-to-ceiling windows opening the house up to bushland views.

Such was the influence of Breuer that the house conforms to his binuclear layout, with one arm containing the public areas – the living room, dining room and the kitchen – and the other, the private ones – the bedrooms and bathrooms. Connecting the two internally is the playroom and, externally, a courtyard. Because there are few internal walls, and glass replaces external ones, there is a tremendous sense of openness. For flexibility, a dividing curtain 'wall' can be pulled across to segregate the living area from the playroom. Today, we are accustomed to this flow of one living space to another, but in the Fifties it must have seemed highly unconventional. A design factor the newspapers of the day picked up on was its elevation. Traditionally, houses were solid and grounded while this seems to float, supported by spindly legs and sporting a strange projection to one side – a ramp.

The reason this house has endured stylistically is due to the absolute conviction with which it was planned both inside and out. Take the colour scheme. 'People who live complicated lives (and most of us seem to) cannot be comfortable in a highly colourful interior,' said Seidler in 1954. It is a house where the use of bold colour, neutrals and earthy shades are held in perfect balance. The external mural sets the tone. Painted by Seidler himself, it recalls artists Miró and Calder, whom Seidler later collected, and captures all the colours used in the interior. There are cool greys on the

N

walls, mid-greys in the carpet and deep brown upholstery on the sofa. The floor-to-ceiling curtains, which provide walls of colour when drawn, are bright orange, electric blue and dark brown.

The furniture is very much the epitome of mid-century excellence and was bought (along with the light fittings) in New York before he left, knowing that he wouldn't get what he wanted in Sydney. Plywood DCM dining chairs, designed in 1946 by Charles and Ray Eames, were the result of wartime exploration into the potential of moulded ply. Combined with a chromed steel structure and exposed rubber shock-mounts, the look is industrial rather than domestic. The Eero Saarinen Womb chair (1948) and Grasshopper chair (1947) have a sculptural quality that is a pleasing counterpoint to the linear design of the living room. The much-copied Ferrari-Hardoy Butterfly chair in eye-popping yellow is aptly placed beside the mural where it looks like a 3D extension of the work's black outline and infill of solid primary colour. The built-in furniture was designed by Seidler, but made by another Viennese immigrant, craftsman Paul Kafka. The cantilevered wall cabinet is a particularly contemporary execution, with its combination of black polished glass and matt painted wood suspended on an Atlantic grey painted wall.

The fireplace and balustrade in rough-hewn sandstone are the only point in the precision interior where a sense of the randomness of nature intrudes, directly reflecting the exterior walls and the organic environment within which the house sits.

With materials hard to come by in this period, necessity proved the mother of invention. Seidler used galvanised piping for the handrail, and explored the possibilities of other new materials. The asphalt tiles in the playroom, while deemed less successful because of their lack of durability, have achieved a rich patina over time. Seidler's experimental thinking was particularly successful in the kitchen. It was the last word in kitchen design in its day with *House & Garden* and *Home Beautiful* magazines wowing their readers with the cutting edge labour-saving devices, wipe-clean industrial stainless steel benchtops and coloured glass-fronted cabinetry. Not even the convention of handles was observed – simple circular cut-out shapes in the glass were enough. A Dishlex dishwasher, Crosley Shelvador fridge of grand American proportions, Kenwood Chef Mixmaster and Bendix front-loading washing machine ensured this 'machine for living' had all the necessary cogs in place.

While the bedrooms are small, they are well-equipped and reflect more intensely the colour scheme of the rest of the house. By extending the door cavities to ceiling height, and using sliding doors, the entrance to the rooms feels generous and the outlook onto nature, from every room, keeps them light and airy. In the master bedroom, a deep brown feature wall with flexible wall-mounted light, strong orange curtain, grey fake-fur bed throw and a simple black desk by Paul Kafka combine comfort, sensory pleasure and functionality.

In 1952, the Rose Seidler House was awarded the highest architectural accolade in Australia, the Sulman Medal. The significance is not to be underestimated, with the establishment having been seeking a style to call its own for so long. Seidler's view, according to writer Donald Leslie Johnson, was that his architecture achieved 'not only a total response to Australia but in complete sympathy, created out of the needs of Australia (society), the site (environment) and that it was logical (rational) and therefore suitable'.

While that may be open to debate, what is incontrovertible is that this house was visionary. So many of its concepts are now commonplace, from the importance of aspect and siting, open-plan living and the integrated kitchen to the painted feature wall, the cantilevered cabinet and insistence on well-designed furniture.

This, Seidler's first commission in Australia, was as confident a statement as a young architect could make to establish his credentials, and laid the foundations for his career as one of Australia's most eminent and enduring architects.

The Rose Seidler House is now the property of the Historic Houses Trust, NSW.

A solid yellow door sits in a wall of glass.
The black desk by Paul Kafka is built in and
cantilevered to give a light, open feel.
The view onto the bushland beyond contrasts
the linear measured quality of the
interior with the randomness of its setting.

DETAILS THE ROSE SEIDLER HOUSE

WOMB CHAIR The Knoll Model 70 chair is better known by its nickname, the Womb chair, so called because a person could easily curl up in it in a foetal position Designed by Eero Saarinen, the Womb chair was an extension of Saarinen's earlier collaborative work with Charles Eames for MoMA's 1940 'Organic Design in Home Furnishings' competition. Six years later, while working for Knoll, he chose to exploit the new medium of fibreglass instead of the earlier moulded plywood techniques pioneered with Eames. It is one of the earliest examples of using this material in furniture, but the rough finish needed to be fully upholstered to have an acceptable appearance. The Womb chair has been in continuous production by Knoll since 1940.

KITCHEN The kitchen purportedly cost more to fit out than the rest of the house. It was the last word in new domestic technology combined with easy-to-clean surfaces and cleverly built-in necessities such as the ironing board. The interiors magazines of the day were in awe of the Dishlex dishwasher and the Bendix front-loading washing machine, not to mention the huge scale of the American Crosley Shelvador fridge. Together with the stainless steel benchtop and cupboard doors of coloured glass, it presents a complete design solution to the functional kitchen. Rose Seidler entertained frequently, was an excellent cook and would have made good use of the cutting-edge amenities.

RUSSEL WRIGHT CROCKERY In keeping with Seidler's furniture purchases for the house, the crockery is the ultimate in Fifties modern. While his mother had managed to retain her beloved Viennese tea set and nineteenth century silver cutlery, Seidler acknowledges he 'wouldn't allow my poor mother to have anything in the house not consistent with the religion: modernism'. He bought from America Russel Wright's American Modern crockery and Highlight Pinch line stainless steel cutlery. These crockery pieces, now in the Museum of Modern Art collection, were an example of the affordable decorating aesthetic that Wright championed. Simple and durable with an appealing biomorphic form, they came in a range of mix and match colours Seidler, a purist, opted for white.

DIVIDING CURTAIN The notion of flexible, as opposed to fixed, spaces in the domestic setting has been exploited in Japanese architecture with sliding screens for centuries. At this time in Australia, walls were fixed, rooms had an explicit function and the idea of a variable open-plan space was radical. In this plan the living/dining/kitchen is linked to the bedroom/bathroom area via a playroom zone. A floor-to-ceiling length curtain 'wall' sweeps across and can either extend the living area or create privacy between the bedroom and playroom. The division of public and private spaces is facilitated and enables a response to the changing needs of the occupants.

COLOUR SCHEME For what was considered a 'white box', there is a significant amount and a varied range of colour in the Rose Seidler House. Yet, because it is recurring, it never seems to jar. The brown painted wall is repeated in the asphalt floor tiles, a feature wall in the foyer, the dividing curtain wall and the upholstery on the sofa. Greys feature in carpets, bedspreads and painted walls while orange fabric curtains provide statement-making panels of vibrant colour, inside and out, when drawn in the evening. The colour scheme is at its warmest and most recessive in the bedrooms. The furnishing is spare – a wall mounted reading light, a side table and a Paul Kafka desk in the master bedroom – and each bedroom has an expansive view to the bush outside.

HARDOY CHAIR While credited to Jorge Ferrari-Hardoy, the ubiquitous Hardoy chair (commonly known as the Butterfly chair in Australia) was actually designed in conjunction with Antonio Bonet and Juan Kurchan. All three were partners in an architectural firm in Argentina. Their inspiration came from a nineteenth century British folding chair. Designed in 1938, the Hardoy chair rapidly became extremely popular and the licence to produce it was acquired in 1947 by New York furniture company Knoll. The bent metal rod frame is simple to manufacture and the chair was copied in large numbers. Loved for its loungey abstract shape, it expressed a freespirited modernism reminiscent of the work of Calder, Arp and Miró.

GROUNDED AND LOW-LYING IN THE LANDSCAPE, CONNECTED TO NATURE AND MAKING THE MOST OF WINTER SUN WHILE MINIMISING SUMMER HEAT, THE HOUSE IS CREATED IN MATERIALS THAT HARK BACK TO A MORE RUSTIC AGE.

PREVIOUS PAGES: While the commission was for an American Colonial-style house, Peter Muller delivered a confident design that owed a debt to the work of Frank Lloyd Wright. Acknowledging the Wrightian influence, Muller was also very much his own man and the solutions he found resonated with the Australian landscape. The 'snotted brickwork' was an attempt by Muller to breathe some life and create some texture in the wire-cut bricks his client purchased without his knowledge.
OPPOSITE: The three-dimensional qualities of this house are instantly evident. The strong horizontal planes plus the contrast of solid mass with light areas of glass and timber give it a dynamism and strength.

While the interior has been considerably refurbished, the original exposed timber beams create a graphic statement. Their connection with the external timbers link interior and exterior visually by extending the eye from one space to the other.

AS AN ARCHITECT, PETER MULLER HAS ALWAYS run his own race. His innate affinity with nature and music has shaped his philosophical outlook and created a mindset that is as subtle as it is strong.

This house, in Sydney's Castlecrag, is the first he designed as a qualified architect. As an early example of his work – he was only 24 at the time – it encapsulates many of the preoccupations and ideas that have endured throughout his long career.

Fundamentally, his architecture is known for an organic, romantic quality which works in harmony with its setting and exploits the inherent beauty of natural materials. He is particularly drawn to materials that are modified and enhanced by the passage of time – wood that weathers, stone that melds into the landscape, or copper that gains the patina of age.

While the Audette House is the start of a personal architectural journey for Muller it is also a highly significant house in the development of a distinctive regional Australian style.

Born in 1927, Muller grew up in the Adelaide suburb of Leabrook, where he recalls a semi-rural upbringing. A preference for the countryside over cities is something that has never left him and this longstanding connection to, and love of nature, was fostered by his mother, a keen gardener. He was also clear from an early age of the profession he would join. 'When I was three years old, my mother says I wanted to be an artichoke when I grew up.'

Muller describes the School of Architecture at Adelaide University as more like a technical college. With a hefty dose of plumbing, carpentry and surveying on the curriculum, it lacked any contemporary context for architecture. So while Muller applauds the sound training in the practical aspects and technical knowledge of building he gained, he also admits that '...the consciousness of world architecture did not extend beyond the Greek orders'.

Muller was a quick and clever student, managing to complete a degree in both engineering and architecture in a record four years. In 1949 he moved to Sydney, took a stepping-stone job at Hennessey and Hennessey architects and set about applying to American universities for a place on a master's degree course. Primarily he wanted to travel, and in 1950 was one of six postgraduate students to receive Fulbright Scholarships funded by The United States Educational Foundation. The University of Pennsylvania could accept him immediately (Yale and Harvard had one to two years' waiting lists), and with his first class passage fully paid for, he set off.

Ironically, while studying in the States, he made no attempt to visit the buildings of the great practising architects of the day. 'I never visited a Frank Lloyd Wright building. I never visited a Marcel Breuer building. I just went skiing instead,' he says. In an encounter at the Harvard School of Architecture, the famous Bauhaus architect Walter Gropius quizzed him about Australia, and while Muller can remember him talking about architecture, he confesses it went in one ear and out the other.

A European trip followed – Denmark, Sweden, England, Italy, France and Switzerland – where his memories are of the food, the people, the countryside. For Muller it was the opportunity to soak up the atmosphere and experience new cultures.

In Paris he did pay a visit to one modernist icon. 'I had a look at one of Le Corbusier's buildings and decided I never wanted to see another as long as I lived...I was so shattered and disappointed, I found it so ugly and so bad in detail and so scungy...I never related to his philosophical or social views of architecture,' he says. At this stage Muller may not have had a firm handle on his own philosophy, but he certainly had a highly developed sense of what it was not. On his return to Australia in 1952, two significant things happened. Taking a job at Fowell, Mansfield & Maclurcan to make ends meet, he met a young draughtsman called Adrian Snodgrass, who was to become a lifelong friend. In Snodgrass he had met someone of like mind who could stretch Muller's natural field of interest. For example, he introduced Muller to the extensive works of Frank Lloyd Wright. Where Muller had reacted so negatively to the work of Le Corbusier, with Wright the connection was instant. The simplicity of materials, the love of nature and the harmonious relationship of a building to its site – Wright's principles resonated with Muller's natural leanings.

The second significant event was a commission that would launch his career and oblige Muller to develop his architectural philosophy and translate it into the three-dimensional. Mr Hauslabe owned the Ford car concession in Australia, and was chairman of the Fulbright Scholarship Committee. His stepson, Bob Audette, had bought a beautiful north facing block of land with Middle Harbour views in Castlecrag and wanted to build a family home. Mr Hauslabe's thoughts obviously turned to the intelligent young architect the Fulbright Scholarship had sent to the USA a couple of years before, and reasoned that his Stateside sojourn would have taught him a thing or two about building an American Colonial house. Peter Muller was the man for the job.

Muller tells of laying out the plans on the bed of his tiny Kings Cross apartment and setting up a model he had made himself so that Bob Audette and his wife could walk around it. When they arrived, Muller excused himself to get cigarettes and left them to view the model and plans alone without undue persuasion. While it was nothing like the original commission of a Colonial house, on Muller's return they agreed to build it, on the condition that it passed the CSIRO's sun orientation tests. It succeeded on all counts.

The model reveals the architect's original intent. The main wall was to be of rustic stone used in conjunction with Australian hardwood, treated only with linseed oil so that it weathered to a soft silvery grey. The combination of honest, unadorned materials was to ensure the house, set amongst angophoras, blended into the landscape. In this postwar period, access to building materials was still extremely limited and Muller admits to bitter disappointment when Audette seized the opportunity to purchase cheap, awful red bricks in lieu of sandstone for the façade. 'It was my first house, so in hindsight I should have been more demanding,' he says now.

In order to create texture in the brickwork, Muller came up with a series of innovative solutions. When laying the bricks, excess mortar was allowed to ooze out from between them. When it dried, it gave the wall a rustic appearance. In addition to this technique, which came to be known as 'snotted brickwork', random bricks were raised and slices of terrazzo were inserted. These elements combined to give Muller something of the organic feel lost by the failure to use stone, yet still delivered the form that he intended.

Although the land had no houses on either side, Muller experienced difficulties with its siting. A freeway was planned to run along the northern, water side of the block and so prevented him siting the house as far forward as he would have liked. Hence the Audette House has a strong street presence, unlike the 'hidden' siting of many of his subsequent houses. It is, however, not a mere façade – its three-dimensional quality is one of the defining aspects of the building. While it is grounded and integrated into the site, with the garage disappearing under the living area, it also has a dynamism and strength created by the bold use of horizontal planes floating above the rows of windows.

Muller's plan was radical for the early Fifties. Most houses presented a flat façade to the street with the important rooms – the living room and master bedroom – at the front. Taking its cue from British housing, the rear of the house incorporated the service areas – kitchen and laundry – with little or no thought given to orientation, siting or access to outdoor space. Muller turned

The site for the house was a very beautiful one with a spectacular view. However when Mr Audette had bought the land, a freeway was scheduled to run along the north side of the block. Happily, this didn't eventuate.

The house has many strong, graphic angles. Garden beds were integrated into the original design, such as this one which runs along the windows facing the street.

all this thinking on its head. What is now commonplace was then revolutionary.

There are three strongly defined zones at ground level – the living/study area, the dining area and covered terrace, and the kitchen/breakfast and utility area. They are held together by the first floor bedroom/bathroom level which sits predominantly over the dining/terrace area but also links the other two zones.

There is a satisfying sense of forms echoing one another, of repetition and symmetry within the context of a limited palette of materials. Muller has always had an emotional and intellectual connection with music, particularly that of Bach, and this appreciation has given his work a distinctive rhythm.

The interior of the house has recently been altered but the essence of the plan has been retained. The main living area is large and open-plan, and connects through floor-to-ceiling doors, originally in timber, to a lawn terrace and pool beyond. Again, the Audette House was a significant departure from the prevailing arrangement of space, which tended to be boxy, compartmentalised rooms with little relationship to outside. Hence, the direct linking of interior and exterior spaces was ahead of its time. Timbers running through the living area were extended beyond the glass to join their exterior counterpart and lead the eye from one space to the other. The U-shaped courtyard, pool and spectacular Middle Harbour views created a compelling vista.

Three years earlier, Harry Seidler had completed the Rose Seidler House – an uncompromising residence in the International Style which quickly became accepted as the defining form of modern architectural thinking. What Muller offered in the Audette House was a real alternative, an opposing architectural standpoint. Grounded and low-lying in the landscape, connected to nature and making the most of winter sun while minimising summer heat, the house is created in materials that hark back to a more rustic age. Yet the use of these materials was far from traditional. They were fashioned to create a fully-formed, dynamic aesthetic which enabled a contemporary way of living. It is easy to see the significance of this house and to understand why many architects drove along Edinburgh Road to view first-hand the work of this audacious young architect.

The Audette House is undoubtedly in line with Frank Lloyd Wright's philosophies. Many of Wright's architectural pillars are also those of Muller and he does admit to leaning too heavily on Wright for solutions to problems, rather than for the generation of ideas.

Interestingly, only two years later, Muller's own house, on an awkward site in Sydney's Whale Beach, had moved further from obvious Wrightian devices to take his fast developing philosophies to a new level. The integration of house and landscape allowed for trees to be incorporated into the living area and for rock formations to be preserved. Muller says, 'I was living in the site as well as the house.' It is this house that architectural historians see as his coming of age as an architect, and it is to this day Muller's favourite house, but the Audette House is where the journey began, and for that it is worth celebrating.

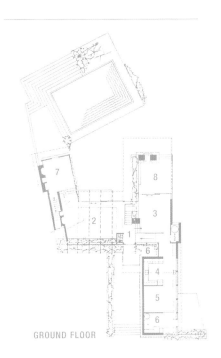

GROUND FLOOR

FIRST FLOOR

N

1. ENTRY 2. LIVING 3. DINING 4. KITCHEN
5. BREAKFAST 6. UTILITY 7. STUDY 8. TERRACE
9. BEDROOM 10. BATHOOM

DETAILS THE AUDETTE HOUSE

EXTERIOR TIMBERS For the exterior timbers Muller used an American product new to Australia. It contained, amongst other things, beeswax and linseed oil, and gave the wood a matt longlasting protective finish that was easy to maintain. The supplier he bought this product from formed the paint and finishes company Wattyl. The exterior woodwork was coated by later owners with marine varnish, giving the appearance it has today. Muller's original finish would have gained a soft patina over time but he recognised that most people want to 'scrape it back and re-marine varnish it every two years to have that fresh, bright, clean look all the time'.

OPEN STAIRS Muller's original design intent was to do away with the small boxy rooms prevalent in the houses of the early Fifties and open the space up in a new way. 'I wanted to eliminate passages,' he says. The staircase, with its open-tread construction, has a feeling of lightness and, as Muller points out, 'allowed one to come in the front door and look completely through it'. The simple 'hung' design, achieved through the minimal use of painted steel, allows the staircase to become inconspicuous, as Muller intended.

SNOTTED BRICKWORK Muller still recalls how devastated he felt when his client Bob Audette bought a job lot of bricks to replace the sandstone intended for the external walling throughout. 'They were wirecut bricks – a cheap, unattractive brick with striations,' he says. In an attempt to bring the bricks to life, Muller devised a technique in which the mortar was allowed to ooze out from between them and harden. This became known as 'snotted brickwork'. Certain bricks were also raised and sections of terrazzo introduced to give a rustic, textured feel to the walls. While it was a clever solution, it never satisfied Muller and he still wishes he had tried harder to talk Audette into using sandstone as planned.

EXPOSED RAFTERS 'I always tried to expose the structure as a sign of integrity,' says Muller. 'By opening up the methodology of construction, there is less need for superfluous decoration.' The exposed rafters in the living area are a strong, graphic element, and the link with the exterior trusses connects internal and external space. The use of a bolt fitting reinforces the sense of honesty, an aspect of Japanese and Balinese architecture that Muller admires. Originally the rafters were Australian hardwood, lightly treated but left their natural colour. but as part of a recent renovation, they have been stained dark grey.

THE ARCHITECT'S MODEL At the age of 24, Muller's presentation of his model of the house was key to securing the commission from clients whose brief was for an American Colonial house. Showing maturity beyond his years, Muller didn't try and talk his potential clients into the project but left them alone to peruse the model. The design differs on a couple of points. Most significantly lost was the rustic stone walled section on the right of the photograph and the long trough for plants which, in the original, fitted neatly under the windows. The trusses, which continued over the roof line, were built as per this design but were removed by a subsequent owner.

THE PLAN OF THE GROUNDS HOUSE TAKES GEOMETRY TO AN EXTREME, AND INVOLVES TWO PRIMARY FORMS – A SQUARE ENCLOSING A CENTRAL, CIRCULAR COURTYARD. TO THE STREET, IT PRESENTS AN IMPASSIVE FACADE OF IMMACULATE PROPORTION.

PREVIOUS PAGES: The exterior of Roy Grounds' 1954 house is an exercise in simplicity. One side of a perfect square faces the street, an oversized door sits centrally and the high-set windows let in light while ensuring privacy. Inside, a cork-tiled wall divides the kitchen from the dining area. The US company Expanko, from which Grounds originally sourced the tiles, again provided imperial measure tiles for the restoration of the wall.
OPPOSITE: The circular courtyard set within an external square illustrates Grounds' preoccupation with geometry. Thirty-two window or door openings onto the courtyard from the house reinforce the connection between the two spaces. Black bamboo acts as a shield from sun, as do the internal bamboo blinds.

SIR ROY GROUNDS WAS A DISTINGUISHED and controversial figure in the postwar Melbourne architectural scene. He had a caustic wit, at times at his colleagues' expense. He once said of his associate Frederick Romberg, 'Freddy's the grain of sand that irritates me to produce a pearl.' From architectural concept to realisation, Grounds was a perfectionist, believing in the power of a single idea, masterfully executed. This award-winning house, built for his wife and family in 1954, is a prime example of his architectural preoccupations at the time, and is commonly viewed as a precursor to his best-known public building, the National Gallery of Victoria.

Even before the Second World War, Grounds began to establish a reputation for avant-garde thinking. He had travelled to London in the late Twenties with his college friend – and later partner – Geoffrey Mewton. From London, they moved to New York where they both worked in architectural firms: Grounds in a practice specialising in Collegiate Gothic and Mewton, at the other end of the spectrum, worked on skyscrapers. Grounds then moved briefly to Hollywood to join his wife, Virginia Marr, and turned his hand to designing film sets for MGM and making furniture in the Bauhaus style for LA's design cognoscenti.

He observed the work of significant American architects practising at the time, such as Richard Neutra, Frank Lloyd Wright and the lesser known William Wurster, who was an exponent of the Bay Area Modern Style. This style emphasised the use of locally found materials with a continuity of indoor and outdoor space through the use of window walls.

In 1932, with his wife and their young son, Marr, he moved back to Melbourne where he designed his first house, known as The Ship, at Ranelagh, Mt Eliza. It had asbestos cement siding with rope handrails and a porthole window lending a nautical air to its seaside setting. The Ship and Mewton's Stooke House attracted attention for their functionalist style, and in 1935 the RVIA (Royal Victorian Institute of Architects) recognised them as notable examples of inter-war domestic architecture. Praise indeed for architects barely 30 years old.

A series of houses designed in this period – the first Henty House, Portland Lodge in Frankston (1933–4), Lyncroft in Shoreham (1934), Fairbairn House in Toorak (1936) and Ramsay House in Mt Eliza (1937) – all show the influence of Wurster. Whether they fulfil Wurster's criterion that a house 'should be an unlaboured thing, that looks as inevitable as something that comes out of the frying pan just right, like an omelette in France', remains to be seen. These are important buildings, with Robin Boyd describing the living room/ kitchen area of the Ramsay House as 'the most important room of the century'.

In 1937, Grounds and his second wife, Betty, spent a year in France, but with the outbreak of war imminent they returned to Melbourne, where they moved into the Ramsay House.

During the war, Grounds was sought out for a new form of commission – apartment blocks – which were to confirm his reputation as one of Melbourne's most notable architects. With a shifting demographic, there was an increasing demand for one- and two-person apartments. Grounds undertook Clendon (1939–40), Clendon Corner (1940),

All the cabinetry has been carefully reconstructed in accordance with the original drawings. A cupboard in limed Victorian ash divides the entrance from the bedroom area. This openness ensures a sense of continuous space. The cabinetry stops short of the windows, allowing that line to remain unbroken.

OPPOSITE: The black slate table (ingeniously engineered to heat up) is surrounded by four MR10 chairs by Mies van der Rohe positioned at the four points of the compass. The hatch in the cork wall allows for easy access from the kitchen. THIS PAGE: Grounds' immaculate sense of proportion is clear from the exact positioning of the timber mullions.

Moonbria (1941) and Quamby (1941) – all of which stand to this day. Here he explored the potential of continuous space, undertaking a considerable level of thoughtful detailing, including retractable ironing boards, fold-up beds and writing desks. The Grounds House in Hill Street is a projection of the line of development he first employed in the design of Quamby flats, also in Toorak. There, the walls form a gently curving arc, radiused from a point some distance from the flats.

Grounds joined the RAAF as a flight lieutenant during the war, and was involved in the construction of airfields and defence buildings. After a brief period of farming postwar, he was appointed senior lecturer at the University of Melbourne in 1948 and was involved in structuring the curriculum. He was a powerful influence on many of his students. Don Fulton, in particular, remembers 'Roy said that a building should have "one simple, strong idea"', a dictum which Fulton followed in his subsequent, award-winning works. Grounds appointed both Frederick Romberg and Robin Boyd as lecturers and, in 1953, they formed the famous partnership Grounds Romberg & Boyd.

Robin Boyd described Melbourne in the 1950s as 'Australia's cradle of modernity', and it was certainly a period of intense experimentation for architects such as Peter McIntyre, Kevin Borland and Boyd himself. Shape and colour, technology and materials, combined with a certain theatricality of construction, all conspired to challenge the establishment. Grounds' use of geometric shapes in plan-form is evident in the designs of the triangular (Leyser) house in Kew (1951)

and the round (Henty) house in Frankston (1952). In fact, the completely circular Henty House II was considered such an unusual building that those driving past it on the Nepean Highway referred to it as 'the flying saucer'.

Early proposals for Hill Street featured three-storey apartments set behind the house. However, the Grounds House, which won the partnership of Grounds Romberg & Boyd the RVIA Architecture Award in 1954, is sited close to the street and was ultimately accompanied by a series of small two-storey town houses staggered behind it, following the slope of the land.

The plan of the Grounds House takes geometry to an extreme, and involves two primary forms – a square enclosing a central, circular courtyard. To the street, it presents an impassive façade of immaculate proportion. The roof is cantilevered with up-sloping eaves, and seems to float above the high windows set just below it. It is easy to see the influence this house seemingly had on Grounds' design for the National Gallery of Victoria (1961–68).

A large front door has Grounds' signature door knocker, and a Japanese maple stands to one side of the slate forecourt. The house is the perfect marriage of forcefulness and elegance, comparable to oriental architecture, where nothing is given away at street level, but also to Palladian architecture, where proportion is paramount.

Entering the house, one is immediately invited into the seemingly large, open living area. Thirty-two full-height windows that form the circular courtyard wall admit an abundance of

light. Each area of the house opens into the courtyard through glass doors. The space is continuous with few interior walls. Those that do exist are clad in vertical ribs of Victorian ash, and frame only the kitchen, bathrooms and children's room. The precision of the design ensures that all joinery, mullions and fitments are set out on radial lines from the courtyard's centre. Bedrooms are closed off by sliding doors, finger-pulled from radial slots, the edge of the door being cleverly disguised among the other ash ribs.

The house has not always been in the immaculate condition shown here. For many years, it was neglected, unloved and its basic design somewhat abused. Fortunately, it was bought in 2003 and painstakingly restored by cardiologist Dr Martin Hiscock. Through original drawings found in the State Library of Victoria, he discovered that architect Don Fulton, as Grounds' assistant, had prepared the 1953 plans. He contacted Fulton, who has advised him throughout the restoration. Hiscock sourced original materials and skilled tradespeople, and also adopted a hands-on approach to the project himself. He carried out the painstaking tasks of stripping the ash mullions and doors of overly heavy liming, laying cork floors and installing aluminium acoustic ceilings in both bathrooms.

'I was determined to restore the house back to its original intention because I think it should never have been allowed to have lost it,' says Hiscock. 'Too often we see architecturally important buildings "improved"…and the whole potency of the original and enduring design is lost.'

The living area has been furnished with design classics in keeping with the era. A pair of Barcelona chairs by Mies van der Rohe with a matching coffee table sit opposite a Florence Knoll sofa. The flamboyant zebra skin rug is a recent addition. Again, cabinetry in the original design has been reinstated along the wall.

Under Hiscock's eagle eye, joinery was expertly reinstated by David Burke, using limed solid timber. Bathroom mosaic tiles matching the originals were found and individually hand-laid in brick pattern according to Grounds' design. A large disc of black slate used for the dining table (the original having been removed from the house) was located in Genoa, Italy, and imported, not once, but twice, due to damage en route. And as per Grounds' design, electrical cable is connected to heat the table in winter. Cork tiles of imperial dimensions from the original company, Expanko, have been used to re-tile the dining room wall with its 'secret doors', and the kitchen restored with the addition of modern appliances, underbench fridges installed and the cork floor returned.

The impressive hand-beaten and rivetted copper flue in the living room has not been replaced by Hiscock, although as with everything to do with the restoration project, he has tracked down its whereabouts. It used to smoke, and discolour the surrounding carpet with embers. One night, during a drinks party at the house, an unfortunate student was given the task of sitting on the roof to fan the smoke and try and increase the draw of the fire!

Heating was originally achieved with Pyrotenax cables laid in the concrete slab, but these had been interrupted over time. Reverse cycle air conditioners, hidden in the living room cupboards, now cope with temperature fluctuations. As architect and writer Neil Clerehan once remarked, the house is a 'fascinatingly detailed treatment of climate and human scale'.

As the courtyard is visible from every room, the use of materials and plants contribute significantly to the ambience of the house. The original Silurian mudstone pavers in the central courtyard had been replaced with bluestone offcuts from the National Gallery open spaces. Hiscock resited the bamboo planting from the south to the north to help screen the living area from the sun. In addition, he removed an unsightly canvas awning and fitted bamboo matchstick blinds to the insides of the windows. On top of that, Hiscock commissioned Don Fulton's son, Simon, to restore the paving to the forecourt.

The use of simple and natural materials, such as Victorian ash, cork, slate and lightly bagged brick walls, recalls the comment of Jennifer Taylor, who said of Roy Grounds' work, 'He combined rationalism and economical planning with a love of warm, natural materials.' There is a Scandinavian feeling that recalls Alvar Aalto's approach to interiors. Hiscock has returned the original aesthetic values of the Grounds House with due regard to heritage principles. Visiting the restored house last year, Lady Betty Grounds exclaimed, 'Why, it looks just like new.' And indeed it does. Having restored the original lustre to this architectural 'pearl', Hiscock reflects, 'This house makes you wonder why we live the way we do, surrounded by four walls covered in Dulux. I prefer to be looking into a garden all the time, thanks; there is a lot to be said for inward looking.'

The Grounds House is celebrated and listed in the Victoria State Heritage Register and classified by the National Trust of Victoria.

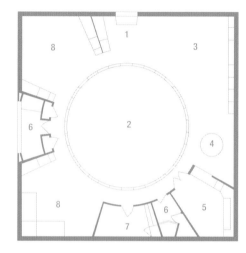

1. ENTRY
2. COURTYARD
3. LIVING
4. DINING
5. KITCHEN
6. BATHROOM
7. GUESTROOM
8. BEDROOM

N

The bedroom is one of the areas with a sliding door for privacy. The treatment of the mix of timbers, from the very fine ribs of ash to the timber-clad ceiling and the limed Victorian ash cabinetry, is resonant of a Scandinavian aesthetic.

DETAILS THE GROUNDS HOUSE

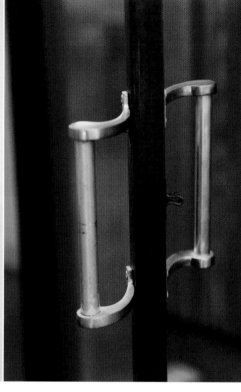

JOINERY The joinery Illustrates Grounds' capacity for complete interior solutions. Sliding timber doors pull out from radial slots to divide off the bedrooms from lobby areas. Clever pie-shaped 'bin cupboards', on each side of the bed in the master bedroom, and the toy box in the children's room provide useful storage. Above, the floating desk is integrated with overhead bookshelves, which house hidden incandescent downlights. These have recently been reinstated, as per the original drawings, by skilled joiners Troy and Lindon Davey-Milne, who worked with David Burke. These limed Tasmanian oak joinery pieces are again set out on radial lines from the courtyard centre.

AWARDS A plaque on the house façade records the 'RVIA Architecture Award Grounds Romberg Boyd 1954'. It was the first RVIA award, and Roy Grounds accepted it from the lord mayor on behalf of the newly formed firm. The house at 24 Hill Street was described by *The Herald* newspaper as 'Victoria's best new building'. The award was not given again until 1963, from which time it was presented as the Victorian Architecture Medal (Bronze). Grounds was later snubbed when, in 1969, a suburban shopping centre won the award over his great work, the National Gallery of Victoria, with the ceremony being held in The Great Hall of the gallery itself.

HANDLES The level of detailing is extraordinary in the Grounds House. Drawings of the courtyard door handles specified their manufacture in cast metal coated with a satin nickel finish, with hand grips of anodised aluminium tubing. They create an elegant sculptural shape, with outside mirroring inside, and folding back neatly when open into catches on the window mullions. All 32 glazed aluminium windows and doors are of the same dimensions, and each of the bedrooms and living areas open into the courtyard.

FOLD-DOWN BOARDS The kitchen, with its bagged brick walls, generous open wooden shelving and benchtops, and stainless steel sink area, is a clean, modern-looking space. Interesting details have been reinstated. Shown here is a fold-down chopping board referred to by Grounds as 'fruit and vegetable flaps'. He used these in the 1940s in the kitchens of the Quamby flats, a project praised for its thoughtful detailing. The handles, by which these boards are pulled down into place, also form their supports in adding an extra useable surface. It is a good example of Grounds' ingenuity and playfulness.

CORK Cork is used as flooring in the kitchen and bathroom but it is its use on the dining room wall that is innovative, acting as a backdrop to the circular, black slate dining table which is screwed into the concrete slab and wired for heating. The cork wall has a hinged serving hatch that Grounds referred to as 'secret doors'. Hiscock reinstated these, cladding them and the wall in Expanko cork tiles. He found the original firm in the USA and imported them so as to be faithful to the dimensions on the drawing which are in imperial (6 inches x 6 inches). Hiscock acknowledges that this restoration project abounded with difficulty and was a 'tricky job' for expert joiner David Burke.

ROOF The original roof was of aluminium sheeting. This was an early use for what was to become a commonly used material for this purpose. Later, the aluminium was replaced with bitumen. The black bamboo can be seen projecting above the roof level. Encircling copper guttering is still in place, and has gained a rich patina over time. Grounds used black bamboo and bluestone pavers again in the courtyards of the National Gallery of Victoria.

'YOU MUST REMEMBER THAT THE POSTWAR NATION FELT AS IF IT HAD BEEN LET OUT OF A BLEAK GREY PRISON, SO WE JUST SPLASHED COLOUR EVERYWHERE, WITHOUT REALLY COMPREHENDING THE SIGNIFICANCE OF WHAT WE WERE DOING.' PETER McINTYRE

PREVIOUS PAGES: The land on which Peter McIntyre built his experimental house in 1955 overlooks the Yarra River, Melbourne. Visible only in winter, the house disappears behind foliage from spring to autumn. The triangular shape of the house is carried through to the windows, and uncompromising colour is used throughout the interior.

OPPOSITE: The entrance to the house is via a set of sandstone steps, the rough hewn quality of which contrasts with the geometric precision of the building. The original panels of red and yellow painted Stramit (a compressed straw material) were replaced with hardwood cladding, and painted a more subdued colour, in the 1960s.

This landing area, with the staircase visible in the foreground, illustrates how the triangular windows create diamond shapes where they converge. The exposed white-painted beams give a linear effect to the ceiling, while the spiral staircase creates a certain dynamism – each contributing its own vibrant geometry.

'THIS PIECE OF LAND HAS DOMINATED MY life,' says architect Peter McIntyre. And when you hear the story, it is true – it has not only dominated his life but shaped his career. The land in question is 1.6 beautiful hectares right on the Yarra River in the Melbourne suburb of Kew. Here in 1955 he built the highly experimental Butterfly House…but before the house came the land.

McIntyre came from a family of architects. His father started a practice in 1921, with McIntyre's uncle joining him in 1930. From the age of seven, Peter McIntyre was running errands and at 13 was doing advanced drawings. By the time his father enrolled him in architecture at 16 (overriding McIntyre's desire to study medicine), he was something of an old hand. Sent out in the spring of 1947 by his father's office to survey a piece of land for a potential client, he spotted the land directly below, which ran beside the river. He slid down on his backside – access was impossible any other way – and was immediately enchanted. 'I had been born in Kew and had grown up swimming in the river,' he says. 'I was absolutely in love with the river, it was everything, and this was absolutely the most fantastic piece of land.'

He asked a real estate agent to find out who it belonged to and approached the owners with all the confidence of a 19 year old without a penny in his pocket!

The land was a leftover part of the Buchan family's subdivision of the Finhaven homestead, a mansion that had been demolished, with parcels of land sold off to create Finhaven Court. This piece of inaccessible land was made even less desirable because the bottom part was subject to flooding, and government plans

from the 1930s existed for a boulevard from the city out along the river. John Buchan, the executor of the estate, was prepared to sell for £100 but needed the agreement of his brothers and sisters. In the meantime, McIntyre would visit the site, and one weekend while surveying it, a man from a neighbouring house asked him what he was doing. They had tea and McIntyre talked about his passion for the land and explained that he was buying it. At the next meeting, John Buchan revealed that the neighbour had offered £2000 for it, having previously offered only £10. McIntyre recounted their conversation and again it went back to the family for discussion. In the end, they agreed to sell it to McIntyre for £400 with a period of six months to pay. He signed a contract on the spot.

When he showed the land to his father, he forbade him to buy it and so McIntyre approached his mentor and friend Robin Boyd. 'Of course Boyd fell in love with it himself. At the time he was running *The Age* Small Homes Service and gave me well-paid work doing amendments to working drawings and perspectives of new houses. I worked night and day, didn't attend lectures and eventually wore myself out and had to go to bed, sick. My parents found out and my father agreed to pay off the balance, making me work the amount off in his office. I had the land but couldn't do anything with it.'

That was all to change with the winning of one of the most prestigious commissions in Melbourne at that time – the Olympic Swimming Stadium – and the land played a role here too. Graduating students in that postwar period seized the opportunity to travel to Europe, Canada

and, if they could, the USA. All McIntyre's year went off on the grand tour, but as he was still paying for the land, he couldn't. It did mean, however, that he, along with ex-serviceman Kevin Borland, John Murphy and John's wife, Phyllis, entered the competition for the Olympic Pool. 'It was in my final year when my lecturer Norman Mussen introduced me to prestressed concrete construction and how counterbalancing forces could make economic sense,' says McIntyre.

On the judging panel were fans of their proposed scheme: Robin Boyd, who defended the aesthetics of their plan, and Professor Francis, in charge of engineering at Melbourne University, who confirmed that it was viable. The scheme utilised high tensile steel post-tension under the guidance of the very experienced structural engineer Bill Irwin. McIntyre is the first to admit the concerns of the architectural establishment around this young team. 'They did indeed query if we were old and experienced enough to do a structure like that, to pioneer that type of construction and to guarantee that the whole thing would stand up.' So many dimensions were a given – pool size and seat size – that new thinking was essential to deliver a workable building while significantly reducing the tonnage of steel required in a time of material shortages. 'Melbourne City Council refused a building permit and we had to go to Sydney to the Building Research Station to have the structure assessed and provide building permits. We had to fight all the way.'

While this significant commission kick-started McIntyre's career as a young gun of the Melbourne architectural scene, it also provided funds to enable him to build

a house on the land in Kew. Working in the offices in St Kilda at that time was a final-year architecture student, Dione Cohen. She helped with the drawings for the house, and one day asked McIntyre who was going to live in it. His response was to ask her to accompany him to Fawkner Park, behind the office, where he said, 'Why don't we live in it together?' Recently, at their 50th wedding anniversary, they went back to the same park bench to 'plan the next 50 years'.

The house itself is extraordinary and experimental. Putting to use many of the things learnt from the Olympic Swimming Stadium experience, and using the same engineer, Bill Irwin, the house is described by McIntyre as an 'A-frame double cantilevered truss. Cantilevered in one direction and then balancing that cantilever with the other direction. Essentially putting one force against another.'

The site was difficult to access and in order to build effectively, explains McIntyre, 'there was no structural member of the cantilever truss any larger than three inches [7.5 cm]. We were able to fabricate it on the ground in small sections, bring it up by hand, lay it on the side of the hill, bolt it together then stand it up and roll it out.' The steel frame was filled in with Stramit, a material made of compressed straw, and the surface painted with polyurethane paint in shades of red, yellow and white. 'You must remember that the postwar nation felt as if it had been let out of a bleak grey prison, so we just splashed colour everywhere, without really comprehending the significance of what we were doing.' What the vibrant colour and unusual shape did was attract lots of attention. The day they

OPPOSITE: The spiral staircase, against the strong wall colours and ceiling timbers, brings to mind a Russian Constructivist painting. THIS PAGE: The kitchen, open to the dining area, uses the same bold colour palette for cupboard doors and inside of the shelving. A Clement Meadmore Cord bar stool sits by the breakfast bar.

moved in, a feature appeared in *The Herald* newspaper and by Saturday morning hundreds of people were coming down the driveway to have a look.

Finished in December when the foliage protected the house, it was a different story come autumn. Suddenly it was exposed and highly visible from the tram that passed over Victoria Bridge. People would rush to the tram windows to speculate on what sort of a building it was.

Dramatic and radical from the exterior, it did, however, prove to be a difficult house to live in. McIntyre is the first to admit its shortcomings. 'Most of the top room was glass to let in the northern sun and boy, did it do that. It also let the cold in as the glass froze – it was like living under a refrigerator. I had to reduce the size of the skylights, insulate the floor and in the early Sixties we clad the outside in hardwood. It was a gradual process of overcoming the inexperience.'

It is important to remember that McIntyre was only 26 when he started designing this, his fourth house. He was also a bachelor with no idea that the house would eventually become home to himself, his wife and four children.

The A-frame construction houses two levels of living space which pivot around a spiral staircase, and allow for generous decks at either side. The rooms are small, but the setting among the treetops is always evident. The triangular form recurs in windows, giving a faceted appearance to interior spaces and, in its highly coloured original state, it is easy to see why the house was compared to a Paul Klee butterfly.

The interior sports glossy red cabinetry in the kitchen and bathroom (which originally had two bathtubs) and bold

yellow walls echoing the colour schemes of Charles and Ray Eames. In fact, the house was furnished with the classic Eames lounge chair and ottoman alongside Australian designer Clement Meadmore's metal and string stools, and Contour chairs by Grant Featherston.

As McIntyre learnt, the difficulty of being at the cutting edge of design was a worrying lack of commissions. He designed a house in Ivanhoe in 1953 for Hans and Pam Snelleman, who still live there today and continue to love what McIntyre did for them. But by 1960 he had no work, so travelled overseas. 'I realised after winning the pool and doing experimental things, that I really had tickets on myself. I thought it was everyone else's fault that I didn't have work. Travelling made me realise what a small fish I was. I had to go away in order to see it. To see how inexperienced I was.'

When he returned, it was with the resolve to change direction and learn more about the building trade. In the following decade he created an extremely large, successful practice that won many prestigious awards.

This house has survived because it was on land that Peter McIntyre has never left. Other houses, all within the McIntyre family, now share the site but the A-frame house is testimony to a time of optimism and spirit of experimental thought. In his book *Australia's Home*, Robin Boyd sums up the house with a wonderful description. 'The home of architects Peter and Dione McIntyre on a precipitous bank of the Yarra...symbolised the spirit of the new Melbourne house in the mid-1950s... Form and colour raised the spirits of the converted and deliberately jarred the unconverted into recognition that war was declared on conservatism.'

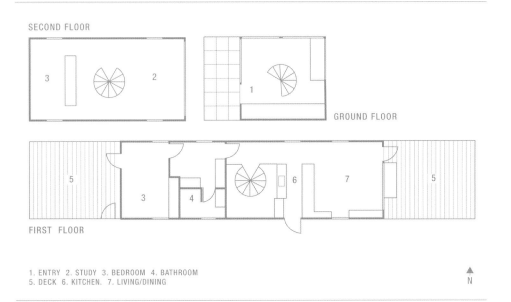

SECOND FLOOR

GROUND FLOOR

FIRST FLOOR

1. ENTRY 2. STUDY 3. BEDROOM 4. BATHROOM
5. DECK 6. KITCHEN. 7. LIVING/DINING

N

The design of the back of the house echoes
the front, and clearly shows the slope of
the roof line to the cantilevered deck beyond.

CANTILEVERED BALCONY McIntyre's award-winning submission (with Kevin Borland and John and Phyllis Murphy) for the 1952 Olympic Swimming Stadium relied on new thinking in terms of structural engineering, which they studied under Norman Mussen. Mussen died and Bill Irwin was the expert who helped the young team navigate the building process. When it came to his own home, McIntyre again worked with Irwin. Set into its triangular frame were two compact storeys with decks on either side forming the extended base of the triangle. Cantilevering out 12 metres, 3 metres above ground level, the decks illustrate the combination of lightness and strength that define the building's construction.

SPIRAL STAIRCASE As with the rest of the building, the structure of the staircase is exposed, and its dynamic design imbues it with a sculptural quality as well as a functional purpose. The treads, handrails and central column are made entirely in steel. 'It was sculpted on site by Arthur McKinna, a remarkable man, half sculptor, half steel fabricator,' says McIntyre. 'I designed several houses around Arthur's skill at steel fabrication. He was responsible for the whole steel frame of the building, which was also completely manufactured on site from small steel members no larger than three inches [7.5 cm] wide.'

EXTERIOR CLADDING McIntyre's interest in new construction methods was matched by a desire to try out new materials. 'We were all carrying out experiments at that time,' says McIntyre of his contemporaries Kevin Borland and Robin Boyd. For this building, McIntyre used panels of Stramit, a compressed straw product '...which on the building's completion in 1955 were painted in the vibrant colours of the new Tip Top ice-cream range', says McIntyre. While it was experimental, it was not enormously functional and the house was very cold in winter. In the 1960s, hardwood cladding was added externally and painted Brunswick green tinted with creosote. 'It was a gradual process of overcoming the inexperience,' says McIntyre.

TIME-LIFE CHAIR Originally designed in 1960 by Charles and Ray Eames specifically for the Time-Life Building lobbies, the chair was put into general production by Herman Miller in 1961. Billed as 'executive seating', the Time-Life chair had a plywood structure wrapped in leather, with upholstered seat and back cushions and polished cast aluminium base and arm supports. Later, an executive desk chair version was also introduced with some small modifications. In 1972, American chess grandmaster Bobby Fischer requested the Time-Life chair for a match against Russian Boris Spassky in Reykjavik. Spassky then wanted one too and Herman Miller had a free TV campaign.

ORIGINAL DRAWING Often referred to as 'the Butterfly House' (an issue of *Vogue* compared it to a Paul Klee butterfly) due to its colourful patterning and spread wings, McIntyre's original drawing shows the house in the natural riverbank setting on the Yarra. Everything about the design spoke of daring, and a strong desire in the postwar period not only to break with the past but to challenge it. The bold geometry of the structural design is emphasised by the use of block colour in primary shades. This contrast of a man-made structure with its natural setting is very obvious in winter when the trees lose their leaves. In summer, however, the house disappears into the foliage.

KITCHEN The galley kitchen, open to the dining area and cantilevered deck beyond, remains completely intact. It has been simply built with a range of open and closed shelving that echoes the original exterior colours. High gloss paint in fire-engine red, canary yellow and black have been used on the backs of shelves and on cupboard doors to create a measured geometry of rectangles and squares recalling Mondrian. The bench in the foreground forms a breakfast bar, and four early Clement Meadmore Cord bar stools sit along the bench on the dining room side. Access to the rear of the house is via a glass door from the kitchen.

THIS HOUSE IS MODEST AND FUNCTIONAL, IT IS HUMAN AND NURTURING, AND HAS PROVIDED WARMTH AND SHELTER TO JACK AND HIS FAMILY FOR 50 YEARS.

PREVIOUS PAGES: The Jack House faces away from the street and onto the bush. It was designed with such sensitivity to the site that little by way of vegetation had to be moved to accommodate the building. A detail of the wallpaper, chosen by Russell Jack and his wife, Pamela, for the dining area
OPPOSITE: The approach to the house is through an arch in a wall and along a timber walkway to the front door.

WHILE WATCHING HER SEVEN-YEAR-OLD grandson playing with his building blocks, Russell Jack's grandmother commented, 'That boy will be an architect.' She was spot on. 'I never wanted to do anything else. Not so much from the design perspective, I just always loved building things. I went to carpentry classes and closed in the back veranda to make myself a bedroom when I was 14,' says Jack.

He received a sound education at Scotch College in Melbourne and Knox Grammar in Sydney and, at the age of 18, enlisted in the RAAF. He acknowledges he went from the rather rarefied atmosphere of an upper North Shore boys' school into the cut and thrust of the forces but managed to stay true to his calling with correspondence courses in several architectural subjects.

In 1946, Jack enrolled at Sydney Technical College, and his time there was important to his career on several counts. 'The course was certainly practical, and the academic side erudite. One academic tutor, Harry Foskett, was quite brilliant and inspired everybody.' Jack worked simultaneously in the offices of Rudder, Littlemore & Rudder, gaining practical, hands-on experience. Most importantly, at STC he met and struck up a great friendship with John Allen, with whom he was later to go into partnership. Together they formed what was to become one of Australia's most significant architectural firms, Allen Jack + Cottier, which has been responsible for a range of high profile projects in Australia and overseas. (Keith Cottier became a principal in 1965.)

But the story of this house is the very opposite of international building contracts and multimillion dollar commissions. This home is modest and functional, it is human and nurturing, and has provided warmth and shelter to Jack and his family for 50 years.

In 1952 Jack won the Byera Hadley Travelling Scholarship; the topic for his studies was, fittingly, related to human expression in contemporary architecture. At this time the rather opposing ideologies of Le Corbusier (the white modernist box) and Frank Lloyd Wright (an organic connection to the site) were the prevailing architectural influences. In London Jack caught the tail end of the Festival of Britain, where he was pleased to see that modernism and decoration could get along perfectly well. He worked for a London architectural firm, Tripe & Wakeham, before returning to Sydney in 1954 with Pamela, his future wife. In 1956, he set up the partnership with John Allen, and built the Jack House the same year. When it won the prestigious architectural prize, the Sulman Award, in 1957, it gave the firm's reputation for innovative work a great boost.

'This land was the last undeveloped block on the street. They just couldn't sell it because of the steepness of the site and the creek running diagonally through it,' says Jack. While the current siting of the house seems the inevitable choice, the first plan was very different. 'The original house Pamela and I designed was steel framed and ran down the western boundary, elevated above the ground with the other wing running east-west. It went to tender but was too expensive and had to be abandoned. In despair, sitting in a restaurant one evening, thinking what to do, the idea just materialised on the back of an envelope. My wife said we should think about timber framing and so we did,' recalls Jack. 'I don't think the other design would have had the same human feeling that this has.'

In the Fifties, some councils made attempts to govern aesthetics, and occasionally flat-roofed houses failed to get planning permission. Then there was the division between 'brick and tile' areas, deemed to be more upmarket, and less salubrious areas, where fibro and weatherboard were still acceptable. The Jacks were fortunate. While the other side of Boundary Road was 'brick and tile', theirs fell into the less rigorously policed category, and so the council had no issue with either the design of the building or the materials used to achieve it.

Interestingly, it is easy to miss the Jack House as you drive by. It doesn't declare itself obviously as part of the streetscape but, rather, is oriented away from the road and towards the bush. According to Jack, 'the prevailing style was for little brick boxes with the important rooms – the living room and the main bedroom – at the front irrespective of aspect or privacy. The accepted thinking on living style was very different from our own. We had to convince lots of our clients that it was the right thing to do. We believed passionately that it was, and having

RIGHT: The wallpapered wall divides the dining area from the kitchen. CENTRE: The tiled area was originally an external space but, as the needs of the family grew, it was enclosed to create another room. FAR RIGHT: The study combined another wallpaper design with built-in shelving and a strong hit of colour.

built this house, they could see what we were talking about.'

What you do see, set back from the road, is a wall with decorative, bagged and painted brickwork. This wall is one of the things that makes Jack's quiet independence of thought apparent. The International School would have designed a precise, unadorned white wall of immaculate proportion, while the typical Sydney School architect would have left the bricks self-finished, as the kiln had produced them. Jack did neither, and the result adds texture and interest to a large surface area. The wall is surrounded by a slim band of windows on both sides and along the top under the eaves. This visually lightens the density of the wall, especially at dusk when lights are on inside.

The other contentious decision was the arch opening in the brickwork that forms the entrance to the house. At the time it was considered reactionary by Keith Cottier, amongst others. Modernity demanded right angles. To this day, Jack defends its appropriateness. 'The logical, natural opening in a brick wall is an arch,' he says. And there is not only one; a second, small-scale arch sits next to the main one, acting as a passage for the stream to run from one side of the wall to the other.

'The main thing to govern my thinking was that the building had to work – it had to be functional,' says Jack. It has a simple L-shaped plan; turn left from the

The wall that faces the street is surrounded by a strip of glass to lighten its appearance. The bricks have been arranged in a repeating pattern to create decorative interest in what would otherwise have been a large plain surface.

front door and you are in the family spaces – the dining room, living room, kitchen and study. Turn right and you are in the bathroom and bedroom wing.

'It was an economical house, there is nothing extravagant about it,' says Jack. 'In the early days, our clients didn't have a great deal of money either and this house could grow and expand.'

Internal walls were non-structural to allow flexibility in the future. And, indeed, the house has developed with time and a growing family. A veranda between the main living area and the study has been closed in and two bedrooms added. An exterior wall of grey, beautifully weathered timber now forms the interior wall of the main bedroom area.

While the purse strings were tight, the ideas were expansive. 'The other thing we tried to do was make it as psychologically big as possible – the free-flowing plan and the floor-to-ceiling glass meant the rooms were never boxes. There is privacy to the street and the rooms themselves are open to the bush,' says Jack.

The space is continuous with no connecting doors but is still broken up into specific rooms. 'I like to be able to live in different spaces, not one huge space. Initially there was no door on the study – until the children came along.' Ever practical, Jack remarked of the dining room, 'It is only used for an hour a day so it makes sense to use it as a thoroughfare.'

Linking the indoor and outdoor spaces was also integral to the scheme. The house was carefully sited, facing north, with minimal vegetation disturbed to accommodate it. The roof and floor planes extend beyond the glass line to

increase the sense of space and create unity, while the same materials were used inside and out. As Frank Lloyd Wright, Jack's hero as a student, wisely said, 'I knew well that no house should ever be put on a hill or on anything. Belonging to it. Hill and house should live together each the happier for the other.' This applies very directly to the Jack House and its surrounds.

But it is not so much Wrightian principles that inform the design itself, but rather a mix of influences, from Japanese traditional houses to Alvar Aalto and, closer to home, one of the pioneers of Australian modernism, Sydney Ancher. Sydney Ancher's beautifully open house in Neutral Bay, and Bill Lucas's Glass house in Castlecrag were both finalists in the Sulman Award the year the Jack House won.

'The expression of the structure is important. It is there for all to see,' says Jack. The exposed post and beam framing and the unpainted woodwork speak of the honesty of the building and also create its enduring appeal. The non-standard windows are generous and proportionally pleasing and allow the outside in.

It is a robust house that has weathered the years well; it is unfussy but, unlike many of his contemporaries, Jack does not shy away from pattern. One of the appealing aspects of this house is the original wallpaper in the study and dining room. Jack is unable to recall whether it was he or Pamela who chose the wallpaper but it serves to emphasise the fact that 'Pamela and I were so much of the one mind that with any disagreement about what to do in the house, the compromise was always better than what either had originally wanted.'

The publicity in the wake of the Sulman Award created a groundswell of public interest and the Jacks often found people peering in from the courtyard. Their neighbour jovially suggested he set up a lemonade stall for the thirsty onlookers. They were not all fans, and one woman wrote to the press saying that to give an award to a house that looked like 'a series of hen coops on sticks' was a disgrace.

Yet the house attracted clients of like mind. Artist Tony Tuckson and his wife, Margaret, commissioned a house in the early Sixties and as Jack says, 'They didn't so much choose an architect as a house.' Margaret Tuckson looked at two of Jack's houses and knew he was the man for the job. She has been there for nearly 50 years, so her instincts were right, and she continues to acknowledge that it is 'a truly wonderful house'. It is modest and unassuming, on a battleaxe block, and you need to be invited to know it is there at all. She tells of a visiting curator, a young man who, after an hour there, declared that he loved it more than any house he had been in. But then it is partly because house and owner are so in tune with one another.

In her book, *An Australian Identity: Houses for Sydney 1953–63*, Jennifer Taylor discusses the work of Russell Jack as creating 'easy and elegant' environments. She goes on to qualify 'easy' as requiring little maintenance and an ability to accept the demands put upon it. 'Elegant' equates with restrained, human and compatible and the result of the use of natural materials. There is then no greater accolade for an architect whose primary aim is that 'it works superbly'.

1. ENTRY 2. BEDROOM 3. LIVING 4. DINING 5. KITCHEN 6. TERRACE (now enclosed)
7. STUDY. 8. BATHROOM/LAUNDRY 9. DECK 10. COURT 11. CARPORT AND TOOLROOM 12. STORE

N

Timber-clad walls in red mahogany impart a rich character to the interior spaces. Classic furniture choices mix with ceramics and wallhangings to create a warm, humanising atmosphere characteristic of Jack's approach to life and architecture.

DETAILS THE JACK HOUSE

ARCHED ENTRANCE In 1956, when the Jack house was built, some architectural devices were not considered appropriate by architects at the vanguard of modernism. The arch was one such form. While considered reactionary by some, Jack found it entirely suitable. It was the logical, truthful way to form an opening in a masonry wall since it needed no overhead support. The house is designed to turn away from the street and face the bush, and the passage through the arch takes the visitor from the public nature of the street into what feels like a secluded, private world.

KITCHEN Jack points to the economy of the house, and the kitchen is a good example of its beautiful, measured quality. Located at the rear of the dining room, it is a very simply designed, functional space. Along the back wall is a row of high cupboards in maple veneer, below which is a slim bench with a stainless steel sink and white Formica benchtop. Underneath, and running the length of the wall, is an open shelf which provides storage for crockery and serving bowls. The spacing of the cabinets and their relative depths is proportionally pleasing.

TIMBER SCREEN Jack has cited a number of influences from Alvar Aalto and Frank Lloyd Wright to Japanese traditional buildings and landscape, drawing on different attributes of these architects or architectural styles to suit his needs. He also felt that the contemporary minimalism needed humanising, and restrained decoration was one way of achieving it. The timber screen outside the main bedroom is functional in that it provides privacy, but is also decorative since the battens vary in height and thickness. Foliage and sunlight create a dappled play of light which subtly enhances the link with nature.

KJÆRHOLM CHAIRS Designed in 1955, the PK22 is arguably the most famous of Kjærholm's creations. Made in satin finished stainless steel and with a one-piece seat of leather, canvas or wicker, the PK22 embodies Kjærholm's obsession with fine detail and a love of the combination of industrial materials and high end craftsmanship. It revolutionised Danish furniture design partly in that it was made of metal at a time when Denmark was defined by hand-crafted timber furniture. The chair won the Lunning Award in 1958. The Jacks' PK22s were bought from Artes Studio in Sydney at a hefty discount due to some marks on the leather. According to Jack, Kjærholm's pieces were so expensive they wouldn't have been able to afford them otherwise.

SHELVING Designed by Jack, these shelves have a simple graphic quality. They are located in the living room and were a later addition as the house evolved and the needs of the family changed. The brackets are manufactured in steel and painted black, and the shelves are supported on little brass pegs. Deep teak shelves house books and journals, and the ceramics that Pamela Jack, a keen potter, collected. The lining boards to which the shelves are attached are red mahogany (a timber Jack used both inside and out), which have been oiled but are otherwise untreated.

SAFARI CHAIR Based on an old colonial chair used by the English in India, variations of the Safari chair have been manufactured all over the world. The most acknowledged version was designed by Danish designer Kaare Klint in 1933. The main features of this chair are its articulated backrest and knockdown construction – it rolls up to just a bundle of sticks weighing 6.5 kg. Australian versions, like this example by John Duffecy Furniture, were produced throughout the Sixties and Seventies. This version returns to a more nineteenth century leg style and, unlike Klint's, has no seat cushion. It suits the simplicity of the Jack House, sitting in front of a timber-clad wall under a portrait of Pamela Jack.

IT IS NOT HARD TO SEE WHY VISITING
JAPANESE ARCHITECTURE STUDENTS
IN THE LATE SIXTIES IDENTIFIED
STRONGLY WITH ITS AESTHETIC
AND WHY AN APPRECIATION OF
BOYD'S WORK DEVELOPED IN JAPAN.

PREVIOUS PAGES: From the street there are only glimpses
of the house situated behind an enormous pine tree
that was on the land when the Boyds bought it in 1957.
At the entrance, the door knocker, which combines
with the house number, sits alongside a discreet name
plaque. OPPOSITE: The main living area is decorated
simply with furniture designed by Boyd himself, and a
button-backed two-seater sofa by Grant Featherston. The
bagged brick walls are painted a warm mottled grey and
the boldly coloured carpet was chosen by Patricia Boyd.

Looking back towards the street, something of the structure of the house is revealed; notably, the ceiling with its woven steel cables overlaid with timber boards, and the windows set under the eaves, which allow natural light into the bathroom (behind the jarrah-clad wall) and beyond into the living area.

NOT ONLY WAS ROBIN BOYD A PARTNER IN one of Melbourne's leading postwar architectural firms, Grounds Romberg & Boyd (or Gromboyd, as it was wittily known), but he was also a highly respected architectural critic and social commentator. It is no surprise then, given his facility with words, that he once described with great clarity what it is for an architect to be his own client. 'In his own home all his philosophy of building must surely blossom, if ever it is so. Here he is both playwright and actor, composer and executant. What manner of architect he is will be laid bare for all the world to see...'

Examining Boyd's Walsh Street residence does just that – it illustrates many of the traits that define one of Australia's most influential architects of the period.

In 1957, Boyd and his wife, Patricia, had just returned from a year-long trip to the USA. As a visiting professor to the Massachusetts Institute of Technology (MIT), Boyd had the opportunity to reconnect with architect and Bauhaus movement founder Walter Gropius, whom he had written about in 1953, and to meet other luminaries of American architecture such as Eero Saarinen, Mies van der Rohe and Frank Lloyd Wright. (It is worth noting that Boyd's erudite writing on Gropius' work ensured an ongoing friendship, and Gropius was to champion Boyd in years to come.) Boyd even had the opportunity to attend an American Institute of Architects (AIA) convention where he noted that all the influential architects spoke with a European accent, confirming the significance of émigrés on the US architectural landscape in the 1950s.

Returning to Melbourne from the States, the Boyds were keen to move to a more central location than their house at Camberwell. Patricia saw a newspaper advertisement for land for sale in the upmarket suburb of South Yarra. The owner, Mrs Bishop, anxious about rising land taxes, was keen to subdivide her property and sell the long, narrow block that was originally the rose garden. Boyd, no stranger to awkward sites, saw the land, bought it on the spot and designed this, the second house he had built for himself and his family.

An early proponent of modernism, he saw the technical developments in materials and engineering as the way forward. It was with a great sense of optimism that he talked about the ability to 'make great open spaces without visible means of support, to throw out parts in cantilever and to open up entire walls to the outdoors through sheets of glass'. But Boyd was also very grounded in a belief that well-designed, functional housing was for all, and a decade earlier had devoted many years to the development and operation of the highly successful Small Homes Service, run by the Royal Victorian Institute of Architects in conjunction with *The Age* newspaper.

Opening postwar in 1947 with Boyd as director, the service offered 40 different house plans for sale at £5 each. An astonishing 1000 plans were sold, mostly to young couples, in the first nine days, and by 1951 the service was providing plans for more than 10 percent of all new housing in Victoria. From 1948, Boyd wrote weekly articles for *The Age* newspaper, which served to increase his public profile. Recruited as a lecturer by Brian Lewis, professor of architecture at the University of Melbourne, Boyd was immersed in architecture in all its facets – practising it, teaching it and writing about it. In 1952, he published his second influential book, *Australia's Home*.

Boyd's work was primarily residential and it is said that he yearned for those large-scale commissions that gave broad recognition to an architect's career. In 1953, when he was on the jury to select a design for Melbourne's Olympic Pool, he championed his friends and contemporaries Kevin Borland, Peter McIntyre and John and Phyllis Murphy in their submission. Genuinely thrilled at the successful outcome of such a bold, modernist scheme, it did cause Boyd, understandably, to question whether his role was always to be that of persuader on behalf of others rather than take centre stage himself.

As an architect, Boyd was a subtle practitioner. In fact, writer Peter Blake commented that his houses were often 'almost invisible from the outside: it was the quality of the space inside that counted not some heroic architectural gestures towards an impressionable world'.

In Boyd's Walsh Street House, there is little sense from the street of what lies behind, as it turns its back to the road and looks inward. A wall with some high windows set behind a majestic pine (that Boyd was at pains to retain from the original garden) is the only visible clue. The house is set back from the street, and wide, open jarrah steps, tapering as they rise to the front door, are protected from the elements by a boldly striped canvas awning. This bridge-style entrance sets the tone for the rest of the house, which feels sensitive and considered, simply designed with a quiet integrity. It is not hard to see why visiting Japanese architecture students in the late Sixties identified strongly with its aesthetic and why an appreciation of Boyd's work developed in Japan.

A red gate and tea-tree fence were added later to stop local dogs using the forecourt as a toilet stop.

Boyd's original plan was for a three-storey house, but having spent one particularly noisy school holidays at home with the children, he radically revised the scheme. In Boyd's own words, this is how the house was planned. 'The device adopted was to divide the house in two by a garden square, forty feet deep, two-storey parents' block at the front, single storey children's block at the back. Tall glass walls, partly obscure, partly hooded, were erected on each side of the garden to protect it from wind and most of the rain, but not sun.'

Boyd's contemporary, architect Peter McIntyre, commented on his 'sheer inventiveness' and his ability as a designer to come up with fresh solutions every time. Walsh Street is a case in point. Its construction can only be described as ingeniously simple. A wall two storeys high at the street side and a lower wall near the rear of the block, where the old rose garden finished at a retaining wall, were connected by woven steel cables, slung between the two. Onto these cables were laid timber boards, butted against one another and held in place with nails pierced through the cables, and bent flush underneath. This innovative tension roof structure was protected externally by a bituminous layer which became molten on the day of pouring. Boyd's practical solution was to add slim timber battens at random to prevent the roof bitumen seeping through any oversized gaps.

In 1947, Boyd had used builder John Murphy to construct his first home in Camberwell, and he was called on again for Walsh Street. A fellow modernist and jazz

aficionado, Murphy was the perfect choice. Boyd left drawings sketchy enough that the council wouldn't ask too many questions, enabling him to push the boundaries of how a home should look and function.

The layout of the house is far from conventional, and must have seemed even more so at the time. It was, however, perfect for the lifestyle of the Boyd family. From the entrance, a long thin dressing room and bathroom lies to the left. Daylight pours in from the row of west-facing windows sitting under the eaves, creating a source of light for both the bathroom and the main living area beyond. Separating these two rooms is a partial wall which stops at the base of the windows. A door in the timber wall leads to the main living area. As with their previous house, Patricia and Robin used this room as a bedroom by night and living space by day – something their friends found highly amusing.

The furnishings are pleasingly spare. There's a bed which becomes a generous day bed with fitted cover and cushions; twin Featherston two-seater sofas with elegant button backs, which moved with them from their previous home in Camberwell; timber bookshelves, which flank both sides of the room, and a cork-topped coffee table designed by Boyd running parallel to an equally long, low sofa. Furniture was always simple and sparely used but very much in the taste of the period. He mixed his own designs with seating locally designed and made by Grant Featherston, alongside the architects' favourite – the Butterfly chair by Ferrari-Hardoy. Art played a big part in the Boyds' lives. Robin Boyd came from a line of distinguished writers and artists and so a variety of artworks decorated the walls.

The kitchen, dining and family room are located on ground level. Limed mountain ash cabinetry faces into the room and was designed to house audio speakers and, unusually for the period, a TV.

In the dining area, 'Winter Triumphant' by Robin's father, Penleigh Boyd, originally hung above the table, while a portrait of Boyd's mother by E. Phillips Fox was placed at the top of the stairs. Work by Arthur Boyd, John Brack, Don Laycock, Asher Bilu, Kevin Connor and Tony Woods added to the artistic ambience of the space.

The colour palette, chosen by Patricia Boyd with renowned interior designer Marion Hall Best, is warm and recessive. The internal rear wall was clad in jarrah boards and left unstained, while the bagged brick has been painted a warm mottled grey. The hit of colour comes from the deep red carpet. The entire breadth of the living area opens to the deck. 'It is a platform independently supported, emphasising that the whole space enclosed here is one, and in it conventional segregations are neither necessary nor desirable,' explained Boyd.

An active couple in the cultural life of the city, the Boyds were very sociable and Patricia was a celebrated cook. This room and deck were the main entertaining area and on one occasion Boyd, standing below, was alarmed to see the degree of flex in the joists and ushered all but 12 guests back into the living room. Apparently, feeling that structural engineers were somewhat over-zealous in their specifications, he was in the habit of reducing their recommendations.

The corresponding room below the living area is the family/dining/kitchen area. A wall of windows facing the garden illustrates Boyd's great sense of proportion. The raw timber beams, treated only with a light grey stain, owe a debt to the Japanese vernacular he admired, while the exposure of the structural elements emphasises the honesty of the building's construction. The limed timber kitchen is discreetly placed at the

back of this space, separated from the main living/dining area by the open-tread staircase and a built-in cabinet in limed mountain ash. The cabinet, facing into the room, was designed to house audio speakers and, radically for the period, a TV set.

While the structure for the adults, family living and entertaining provided the hub of the house, at the opposite side of the block, a single storey building was given over to the children's quarters. It later became known by the children as the 'other side', and at mealtimes they were called from their homework by a short ring on the telephone extension. The children's zone comprised two dedicated bedrooms, a guest room, bathroom and a sitting room/study facing out to the courtyard. The rooms, with the same bagged walls painted warm mottled grey and timber partitions, are simply furnished with built-in desks and neat single beds. Robin's son, Penleigh Boyd, recalls a degree of enviable freedom in having their own end of the house. 'We had our own access through the rear lane, a TV room and study space and a view into the marvellous courtyard. We even had a secret basement which was used for storage. Robin also had a passion for cars and we were one of the first families in Melbourne to own a Citroen Goddess. People looked at it as though it was a spaceship. So, all in all, we were a thoroughly modern family.'

Between the two areas of the house lies a garden. As Boyd said, 'One of the principal objectives in planning was to create a private indoor-outdoor environment despite the narrowness of the allotment and the congested surroundings of an inner suburb.' These days we talk of the courtyard as an outdoor room and an extension of our living space as if it's

Exposed beams speak for the honesty of the building's construction.
The Boyds were great collectors of art and shown here is 'Solstar' by Asher Bilu.

OPPOSITE: Looking back towards the main part of the house, the cables stretching from one structure to the other are visible. The courtyard was Boyd's solution to creating a private outdoor space on a narrow block in a suburban setting. THIS PAGE: The deck extends from the main living space to create an entertaining area overlooking the courtyard garden.

something new, but Boyd had thoroughly embraced the concept in 1958.

The plan for Walsh Street inspired Mary and Grant Featherston to commission Boyd to design their house a decade later. The Featherston House is a tour de force with its completely integrated indoor garden, floating platforms and translucent fibreglass roof.

Boyd's ingenuity, illustrated by the Walsh Street House, is an example of his ability to think laterally, to be aesthetically inventive and to solve problems of difficult sites. The James House in Kew (1956) is semi-underground; the Lloyd House in Brighton (1959) is fan-shaped to work around a pear tree, while the Richardson House in Toorak (1953) was designed as a bridge over a dry creek bed. He produced an enormous range of housing in his career and embraced the possibilities of new methods of construction to realise his concepts. His writings on architecture and society challenged and shaped popular opinion, and his work *The Australian Ugliness* (1960) pulled no punches in its attack on certain aspects of popular taste. A man of principle, he wasn't afraid to take Australia to task, especially in its increasing Americanisation, and endeavoured to make the country strive for its own, distinctive cultural identity.

Internationally, his reputation as a writer grew when, at the recommendation of Walter Gropius, a New York publisher commissioned Boyd to write a short biography of Japanese architect Kenzo Tange. Tange's comment, 'I could not help admiring you for your deep understanding and correct criticism on Japanese culture as well as my own work', goes some way to show Boyd's extraordinary sensitivity and ability to tune in to the work of another architect in another culture. Boyd may have felt disappointed that his career did not embrace large-scale commissions but in many ways he played an even more significant role in the development of Australian architecture. He acted as the gatekeeper for aesthetic standards and played a crucial intermediary role, through his writing, between the profession and the public. As Joseph Burke said of Boyd after his untimely death in 1971 at the age of only 52, he was 'the artistic conscience of his country, in the future of which he passionately believed'.

The Walsh Street House is the property of the Robin Boyd Foundation. The Robin Boyd Foundation has been established by the National Trust of Australia (Victoria).

The study area in the children's section featured the same bagged brick walls and simple functional furniture as used elsewhere. As Penleigh Boyd recalls, there was an enviable degree of freedom in having their own end of the house.

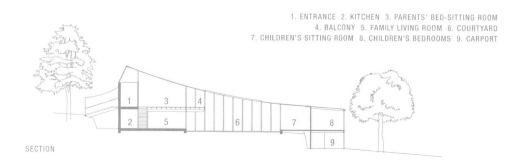

1. ENTRANCE 2. KITCHEN 3. PARENTS' BED-SITTING ROOM
4. BALCONY 5. FAMILY LIVING ROOM 6. COURTYARD
7. CHILDREN'S SITTING ROOM 8. CHILDREN'S BEDROOMS 9. CARPORT

SECTION

DETAILS THE WALSH STREET HOUSE

ENTRANCE Boyd's appreciation of the Japanese aesthetic is evident from the entrance to his house. Despite the modest size of the block, Boyd chose to set the house back from the street to ensure an enormous pine tree, from the original garden, was left in situ. The timber steps are open treads and have a measured, proportionally pleasing quality. In profile, it can be seen that the steps form a bridge from the ground level to the first floor entrance. Simple, circular brass door furniture has the number of the house and the name of its owner engraved in the discs. A striped awning provides protection from the elements.

FEATHERSTON SOFA The R160 lounge chair and the matching R161 settee by Grant Featherston were designed in 1952 and produced until 1956 by local Melbourne manufacturer, Emerson Brothers. Also known as the Contour chair to describe its form fitting shape, the range was a great success in Australia as it encapsulated a 'modern' look seen overseas in the work of Charles and Ray Eames and Eero Saarinen. Using bent plywood, Featherston was able to create a comfortable organic-shaped chair without the traditional bulkiness of upholstered furniture. Grant and Mary Featherston were friends of the Boyds, and Boyd designed a house for them in 1967, in which Mary Featherston lives to this day.

KITCHEN From formal to family room is via an open staircase from the first floor entry level to the ground floor where the kitchen, dining area and family room are located. The kitchen is long and slim, tucked behind the staircase. The rustic effect of the exposed beams is reflected in the treatment of the glazed brick floor. A large throw-down carpet covers much of the brick floor in the dining and living area, but the brick floor was left exposed in the kitchen space, except for a strip of cushioned flooring in front of the appliances. The limed plywood kitchen is economical and functional. It is properly planned with a place for everything – including pots.

BOYD-DESIGNED FURNITURE
In addition to pieces of furniture by
Grant Featherston and Clement
Meadmore, Boyd designed his own
furniture specifically for the house at
Walsh Street, including the long, low sofa
and complementary coffee table. They
are simple, clean designs that reflect the
Fifties aesthetic for streamlined shapes
with little extraneous detailing. The
Boyds, unconventionally, used the living
space as a bedroom by night, but by
day the bed had its own slip cover and
cushions to transform it into a furniture
piece smart enough for visitors.
Celebrated interior designer Marion Hall
Best advised Patricia Boyd on the
interior décor of the house, in particular
recommending the deep red carpet.

BATHROOM
The bathroom/dressing
room is positioned between the wall that
faces the street and the three-quarter
height wall that divides it from the living
room. It is a long slim space naturally
lit by the bank of high windows under
the eaves. Cupboards flank one side,
and a large mirror and basin are built
in on the other. The side wall is a mix
of the bagged brick painted dark grey
on the upper half and mosaic tiles shot
with bronze on the lower half. A large
copper shroud extends to the ceiling
and conceals all bathroom plumbing,
including vents from the kitchen below.

CEILING
It is interesting to see
close-up the structure of the ceiling.
Woven steel cables provide the tensile
strength for the timber boards to be
placed, side-by-side, upon them
and held in place with nails. Slim
timber battens were added at random
during construction to prevent the roof
bitumen seeping through oversized gaps.
The raw timber was left unpainted and
exposed, reinforcing Boyd's philosophy
that the integrity of materials and
honesty of construction should be seen
rather than covered up. The cables
ran from inside to out, through the
courtyard, and were used in the same
way to form the structural support for
the ceiling in the children's quarters.

PART OF WHAT WAS RADICAL ABOUT
THIS HOUSE WAS THE FLEXIBILITY IT
OFFERED, AND WITH IT, A GENUINELY
NEW WAY OF RESPONDING TO LIFE AND
NATURE. MOVING THROUGH IT, ONE IS
WELL AWARE OF THE WEATHER.

PREVIOUS PAGES: The north-facing tiled terrace
adjoins both the living area, to the left, and the
flyscreened breezeway. The use of terracotta tiles
inside and out and the floor-to-ceiling sliding doors
from the living room blur the lines between the
two spaces. Furniture designed by David McGlashan
complements the structure of the building.
OPPOSITE: The entrance to the Grimwade House
illustrates the mix of materials used throughout:
glass, timber, limestone and terracotta tile.
This simple palette of honest, unadorned materials
unifies a series of pavilions and outdoor spaces.

The enclosed courtyard, protected from southerly winds, is an ideal area for outdoor entertaining. The house was designed to accommodate extended family during the holidays; a generous table, sited under a casuarina, is a perfect spot to gather.

THIS IS THE ONLY HOUSE IN THE BOOK CREDITED as the work of two architects – David McGlashan and Neil Everist. It serves to highlight the particular working relationship of this Melbourne/Geelong-based partnership. They met while studying architecture at the University of Melbourne and formed the architectural firm McGlashan and Everist in 1955. Initially McGlashan worked out of a room in his parents' house in Melbourne, while Everist set up in small premises in Geelong, Victoria's largest provincial city, to the south of Melbourne. While they had very different personalities, and worked from two offices, they set up a system of operating that ensured the work of the architectural practice had but one distinctive voice.

Neil Everist explains, '…we developed a series of planning processes and standard details. This meant that the architectural language of buildings emanating from either the Melbourne or the Geelong offices would be indistinguishable, but only one partner would engage with the client.' Ease of communication wasn't what it is today and a combination of sketches sent by train and endless telephone calls meant that the 'best solution' was always the outcome. 'If one of us wanted to alter an approach to a design, change a detail, or overcome a problem, the process was to develop the "best solution"…David always said that if we had any real doubts about a solution, we were probably wrong and should start again,' recalls Everist. The system clearly suited them as they worked together in this fashion for over 40 years, initially on housing and, later, mainly designing

educational buildings, until their retirement in the late 1990s.

Young architects – in the right place at the right time – McGlashan and Everist gained commissions for several holiday houses. A product of peace and prosperity, the holiday house brought with it a certain freedom – a freedom to explore different ways of living and to push the conventional boundaries of what a house should be and how it should function.

In her essay for the exhibition catalogue *Living in Landscape: Heide and Houses by McGlashan and Everist*, Judith Trimble makes note of the connection both architects had as boys to the land, the beach, the light and the water, enhancing their feeling for and 'empathy with the natural environment'. Combined with this fundamental response to sense of place is an understanding of prevailing global trends in modernist architecture and an ambition to create a local response.

In 1959 McGlashan had his first trip to the USA, where he saw the buildings of some of the greats of American architecture – Frank Lloyd Wright, Richard Neutra and Marcel Breuer. Particularly inspiring to McGlashan was the work of Edward Larrabee Barnes and his Platform Houses, which were carefully integrated into the landscape and used pavilions to create a mix of connected indoor and outdoor spaces. Not long after returning, McGlashan cancelled all the firm's subscriptions to overseas architectural magazines. They wanted to create an Australian approach and didn't want to be unduly influenced by what they saw happening at an international level.

The commission that was to change the course of their careers came from the

Grimwade family, who owned a large block of land and an old boarding house in Rye, a coastal town outside Melbourne. Mr Grimwade wanted a house that could combine a permanent retirement residence for himself and his wife with a holiday house for his four daughters and their families. The main house needed to operate independently when guests were not staying but have adequate space readily available to accommodate large numbers to sleep, eat and relax. Ideally it would cater for a degree of separation between adults and children. The needs of their client and McGlashan and Everist's architectural preoccupations could not have been more closely aligned as the unconventional requirements of the house allowed for, even required, a lateral approach to its planning and design.

Siting was a particular skill of McGlashan's and such was his ability that he was often asked to site buildings other than his own work. In this case, the resulting plan includes a number of pavilions, each sensitively sited, and juxtaposed in such a way as to allow courtyards and outdoor spaces to be integrated into the design. The main house forms an L-shape. To the left of the entrance is the master bedroom wing, with four bedrooms and two bathrooms; to the right is the kitchen/living area. Accessed via both the living area and the entrance/breezeway is a north-east facing terrace positioned to maximise winter sun. The smaller pavilions consist of a children's bedroom wing, a rumpus room and staff quarters, between which is a large courtyard where a dining table sits under a casuarina tree.

While it is a large house, its mass is reduced by the modular approach, which McGlashan explained as the plan being 'taken apart', a deconstruction of sorts which allows the components to be arranged in a different pattern.

One of the most significant elements of the design is the treatment of the outdoor spaces. Terracotta tiles, used throughout the main house and terrace, have a unifying effect. As the walls facing onto the terrace are either glazed or flyscreened, each area, internal or external, is permanently visible from the other, and the sense of connection is obvious. The house turns its back to the south to ensure privacy and give protection from the southerly winds.

Also significant to the design is the extensive use of breezeways. The dramatic bedroom wing, which sits long and low on the land, is flyscreened but not glazed along the exterior wall to form an outdoor room. Moving throughout the house, one is well aware of the weather. As Everist points out, space was seldom enclosed but, rather, 'movement is unrestricted and undefined through major spaces'. And part of what was radical about this house was the flexibility it offered, and with it, a genuinely new way of responding to life and nature.

A warm evening and a family dinner can be held in the courtyard, with pre-dinner drinks on the terrace. On a cold winter's night, there is no need to stray far from the kitchen, the sliding doors open for easy access. The human scale of the design allowed for what McGlashan described as 'nearby spaces', and it is easy to understand how so many different activities, across the

generations, could be taking place simultaneously in the house.

The house references Japanese architecture in several ways and, indeed, before designing the Grimwade House, McGlashan was given a book on the Katsura Imperial Villa, a Japanese country house and garden, with a variety of interlocking spaces. Echoes of Japanese architecture are seen in the simple measured quality of the spaces in the Grimwade House; the sliding doors and screens which allow spaces to change and adjust according to the weather or the needs of family life; the connection of the indoor and outdoor spaces, the lightness of the structure and the connection to the site.

And so, too, does the restricted palette of materials. The floors, as mentioned, are terracotta tile, the walls are clad in western red cedar and the ceiling is a cream coloured Vermiculite, to help with the acoustics of a predominantly tiled space. Limestone, quarried on the site, is used for external, and one internal, wall. The house is constructed of honest, natural, warm and unadorned materials.

Adding to the sense of a whole, seamless space is the furniture. When interviewed by Eric Hunter for the TV programme *This Day Tonight* after the completion of Heide II in 1967, McGlashan described furniture he had designed there as 'an organic part of the architectural structure of the house – simple and complete. It fits in, in all respects.'

Initially, the Grimwade House had only one freestanding piece that McGlashan had designed – a large glass mosaic coffee table. He had also designed the low outdoor benches, fixed in place on

The main living area features David McGlashan-designed furniture. The walls are clad in cedar, which is the perfect backdrop for a collection of Aboriginal and Oceanic artefacts.

There are certain vistas where the influence of Japanese architecture is evident. The measured proportions of the windows, the low, fixed seating (also in terracotta tile) and the view to the small pond, surrounded by rocks, impart sensitivity to a Japanese aesthetic.

the terrace. Over the years, other pieces were added and the sense of a complete vision was established. Simple rectangular shapes form tables and bench seating. Steel frames are topped with materials already used in the house such as terracotta tiles for table tops and slim cushion pads on the benches. The McGlashan-designed sofas, originally for Heide II, are based on the same rectangular steel shape, the back and arms formed by simple wooden planks and the webbed frames filled with large comfortable cushions.

While the design of the house is deceptively simple, there is an extraordinary level of thoughtful detailing. For example, a small leather pull handle in a cedar-clad wall is the only giveaway that a generous drinks cupboard lies behind – complete with a small sink, ample cupboards and a shelved wall backed with glass mosaics. The fireplace has integrated storage for logs, and the original mesh curtain fireguard. A large sliding door separates the kitchen from the dining area, and a connecting cutlery drawer can slide either way. However, McGlashan, in particular, didn't like mantelpieces and the Grimwades had an impressive collection of shells they liked to display. The compromise was what came to be known as 'the shell box', a long trough sunk into the tiles at the far end of the living area to house the collection.

Through a family connection, the Grimwade House came to the attention of John and Sunday Reed, who wanted a holiday house designed for a plot of land they owned on the beach at Aspendale, a Melbourne suburb on Port Philip Bay.

The Reeds were art collectors and the kind of unconventional clients who allow young architects to show the extent of their ability. As Everist says, 'The brief was exciting, imaginative and individual, and the site, virtually on the beach, was unique.' They also had another request – that it be finished in 34 working days.

'The Reed's [sic] enthusiastically responded to the developed bathing box concept, and loved the boardwalk and detached wings floating and embracing the sandy dune…this was the trial run and the first base. I was blessed to have clients who would commission my dreams,' wrote McGlashan.

Two glass pavilions – one for living, one for sleeping, connected by a covered walkway – were completed by the Christmas holidays, 1961.

This commission was, Everist feels, something of a testing ground for their next, much more significant project – Heide II at Bulleen, which was awarded the bronze medal of the Victorian Chapter of the RAIA in 1968 'for outstanding architecture'. This has become the firm's most famous domestic residence; the design of a gallery space to be lived in. Everist does however note that in this instance the design relationship was very much forged between the Reeds, particularly Sunday, and David McGlashan. With the brief requiring a romantic building with a sense of mystery, the space and natural light appropriate to a gallery, and the ability of the house to sit in the garden as though itself a sculpture, the commission was a challenge. The outcome, however, was an iconic building that answered every request.

1. LIVING
2. KITCHEN
3. BREEZEWAY
4. SCREENED PORCH
5. TERRACE
6. RUMPUS
7. COURT

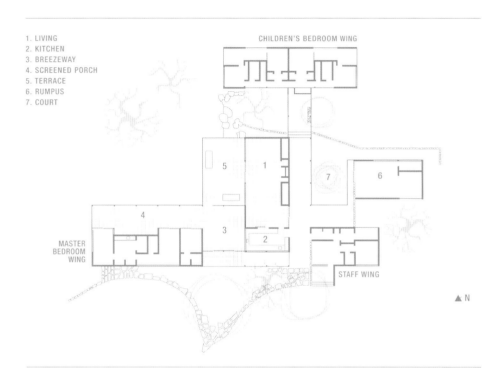

As Professor Philip Goad notes, 'In choosing McGlashan and Everist to design Heide II the Reeds were commissioning a work of art. The Reeds regularly commissioned from emerging young artists. Which is what McGlashan and Everist were.'

McGlashan's view that houses are the 'background for people and the things they have with them' may have a simplistic ring to it. Examining the Grimwade House, which won the Victorian Architecture Medal in 1963, it is clear that McGlashan and Everist, working through their process of 'best solution', explored the potential of their projects from the macro (siting, spatial relationships and materials) down to the micro (how the kitchen drawer operates). Once a building was finished, the level of consideration was such that it became a truly complete space providing functionality, visual pleasure and a connection to nature. And, as architects, having done their job well, it did indeed, as McGlashan said, become the background, the context for living and for living well.

THIS PAGE: The bedroom wing sits long and low on the land, creating privacy for the north-facing courtyard. OPPOSITE: The flyscreened area is essentially a deep enclosed veranda which features a limestone wall, internally and externally. Decorative materials are used sparingly, with one example being the shelf in glass mosaic tiles which runs the length of this space.

DETAILS THE GRIMWADE HOUSE

FIREPLACE The main living area maintains a completely open, streamlined feel with nothing protruding into the room to break up the flow of the space. The fireplace is set into the wall, flush with the cedar panelling above. A deep strip of copper, delineating the area, encompasses not only the fireplace but conveniently placed storage for wood and newspapers on either side. The design included an integrated fireguard in fine mesh which can be pulled across when the fire is lit. While there is underfloor heating in the kitchen and front bedrooms, the fireplace and the natural heat of the sun (which reaches the back wall in winter) are the only forms of heat in the main living area.

SHELL DISPLAY The Grimwades had gathered an impressive collection of local and exotic shells, which had previously been displayed on a mantelpiece. Given the design of the fireplace, a mantelpiece was not considered appropriate and so a long sunken trough at the rear of the living room was the novel solution for the display of the collection. Tiled in terracotta coloured glass mosaic tiles, the design had a small lip to allow a glass lid to sit on top, bringing it flush with the floor level.

CURTAINS The setting for the house is very private, set well back from the road amongst mature casuarinas, and its design mixes communal space and private places with great success. In the living room, there are long fine fibreglass curtains (which have the appearance of rough linen). Mostly the house is open to the landscape. In the bedrooms, the curtains (shown above), sourced in Melbourne, are made from fine bamboo and are in tune with the natural materials used throughout the house. The diffused light they admit is soft and gentle.

KITCHEN The kitchen is large and has two access points to other rooms to allow for maximum flexibility. A large sliding glass window can be opened to form a serving hatch onto the breezeway if the weather is warm and the preference is for dining there. Alternatively there is a generous opening, at bench height, between the kitchen and the dining area in the living room. Here, a wooden panel slides over to close off or open up this connecting space. The kitchen was originally designed in white laminate but was renovated 15 years ago using Tasmanian oak and terracotta tiles which brought it more in keeping with the materials used in the rest of the house.

HIDDEN DRINKS CABINET In line with the seamless nature of the living space is the location of the generous drinks room. The only giveaway that it exists is a now worn loop of leather, set at handle height in the western red cedar panelling. Behind the secret door is a large, walk-in cupboard, also wood panelled, but with a wall of dark aubergine glass mosaic tiles set behind a small metal sink and shelving for glasses. It means that on a cold winter's night one doesn't have to stray far from the fire to fix a whisky and water. Symmetrically placed on the other side of the fireplace is another cupboard for general storage.

BREEZEWAYS Part of the McGlashan and Everist philosophy was to encourage a different way of living. They wanted their clients to experience changes of weather as they moved through the house. The design places great emphasis on the variety of spaces: from the fully enclosed to exterior spaces which are protected but not covered, and spaces which blend the two. The use of breezeways, areas in which two walls are flyscreened but not glazed, gives a degree of exposure to the elements without actually being outside. The bedrooms for the main house are situated along this generous flyscreened veranda and often necessitate additional clothing as one moves from the living room to the bedroom, inviting an acknowledgement of the climate.

'THERE IS A CONCEPT I'D ALWAYS BEEN ATTACHED TO: THE PRINCIPLE THAT TO BE A MODERN ARCHITECT, ONE HAS TO SEVER ONESELF TOTALLY FROM THE PAST AND ASK QUESTIONS AS THOUGH NOTHING EXISTED BEFORE. CANBERRA WAS THE IDEAL PLACE.' ENRICO TAGLIETTI

PREVIOUS PAGES: Taglietti's design for the Dingle House had to accommodate the cross-sloping nature of the land. Set back from the street amongst established trees for maximum privacy, it is the strong use of horizontals that define this building.
OPPOSITE: This generous timber deck runs the entire length of the house and is protected by the deep overhang of the roof.

BELOW: View from the raised living room towards the dining area shows how the two spaces relate. The timber clad section of wall is broken by the clerestory windows which admit light from the west. RIGHT: Looking towards the sliding glass doors which lead to the deck.

ITALIAN-BORN ARCHITECT ENRICO TAGLIETTI and Australia's barely formed capital city, Canberra, found one another in 1955. It was a marriage of person and place that has remained almost unbroken for 52 years and, as with the best of marriages, the influence of one upon the other has been mutually beneficial.

Born in Milan in 1926, Taglietti spent his formative years with his family in Asmara in Eritrea. Moving back to Italy in 1948, he took up architecture at Milan Polytechnic. During this period, he was exposed to the teaching and thinking of Italy's leading architectural intelligentsia. Carlo Mollino, he recalls, 'probably influenced me in relation to Baroque form', which Taglietti qualifies as an intention to 'create *meraviglia*, to amaze the visitor'; Gio Ponti he remembers as being 'so fresh in his approach, so naïve that he had enormous value as a teacher'. Artist Lucio Fontana, whose slicing of the canvas indicated a personality more about action than words, became a close friend. Add to the mix the teaching of Marco Zanuso, Bruno Zevi and Pier Luigi Nervi, and Taglietti's few years in Milan enabled the formation of his enduring philosophy of an organic approach to architecture. In 1954 he attended the Le Corbusier summer school in Marseilles and worked directing the foreign entries at the Tenth Triennale in Milan, which brought him into contact with Aalto, Niemeyer and Buckminster Fuller amongst others. All in all his contacts in the early Fifties are a roll call of the postwar avant-garde architectural set both in Italy and abroad.

The photographs from this period of the Milan apartment he shared with his wife, Franca, reveal a home that is the epitome of modern style. Chairs by Mollino and a table by De Carli are accompanied by Taglietti's own designs of a large honeycomb bookshelf comprising a series of stacked hexagons in blue, yellow and black, and a crafted, sculptural coffee table which owes a debt to Finnish designer Tapio Wirkkala. The apartment not only had style, it had panache.

An opportunity that arose in 1955 was to change the course of Taglietti's life. David Jones, the Australian department store chain, was to host an exhibition in Sydney of Italian architecture, furniture and fashion, and wanted an Italian architect to design it. They first approached Gio Ponti, but it was Taglietti who ended up with the commission. 'My wife and I thought of it as a second honeymoon,' he recalls. The exhibition was a great success, as was Taglietti's relationship with Sir Charles Lloyd Jones, who put him on a retainer. His scheduled stay of six weeks turned into six months. During this time he was sent to Canberra to find a site for a new Italian Embassy and from that moment on, it was to that city he was drawn.

In 1955, Canberra had a population of only 40,000, and its appeal to this architect from the old world was the very new-worldliness it offered. 'There is an old concept I'd always been attached to: the principle that to be a modern architect, one has to sever oneself totally from the past and ask questions as though nothing existed before. Canberra was the ideal place.'

Taglietti is a great lover of the written word and his published work is littered with poems and literary references. The similarity between Canberra, a city without history, and Zobeide, a fictional city in Italo Calvino's novel *Invisible Cities,* was not lost on him. He felt he had found a place untouched by 'ugliness or history'. He embraced the empty spaces and the silence. Socially, however, it was far from silent and Taglietti commented that 'a young fellow arriving from Italy could mix without any problem with the atomic energy scholar, a Nobel laureate and with a Prime Minister' (Sir Mark Oliphant, John Carew Eccles and Sir Robert Menzies, respectively). Taglietti wasn't just any young architect. He would have presented as sophisticated and debonair, well-read and well-connected: a man to whom aesthetics were grounded in an understanding of site, environment, aspect, client and economics. However attractive his attributes and his Italian qualifications, he wasn't permitted to register with the local architectural body and it was through the Department of the Interior in Canberra rather than the Board of Architects that he initially received permission to practice. It's interesting that half a century later, he was awarded Australia's most prestigious architecture prize, the RAIA Gold Medal 2007.

His instinctive response to Canberra and its people was rewarded by dozens of commissions over the years, ranging from houses to embassies, libraries, schools, conference centres and a cinema complex. His many commissions from the National Capital Development Commission include the Australian War Memorial Repository in 1978. He was there at the beginning of Canberra's major growth spurt and shaped the urban landscape of this growing city.

The house shown here is from his early period, and illustrates in a domestic setting many of the preoccupations that were applied in larger, more dramatic scale, in his public works. His approach was always consistent. In his own words, he describes the process of creation: 'First, I develop a brief, speaking with the client, and together with the client I create the basic area requirements...I then transform this floor plan in a volumetric mass and put it in context with the environment and the block of land. At this point I forget the requirements for a moment and consider only the volume. Then I play with the volume. If I cut here, if I add there, I might overhang there. What is the most suitable volume to the particularity of the site, to the orientation, to the environment and finally to the agreed brief.' To realise these volumes his favourite material was concrete for 'its plasticity, its ability to make any shapes or volume and still stand up'.

It is obvious that many of these ideas are at play in the Dingle House. The site was not an easy one – a steep cross-sloping block – but had the appeal of facing north at the rear and overlooking the pleasing panorama of the Federal Golf Course. The house is set back from the road and the façade designed to maximise privacy. No windows face onto the street and even the entrance is tucked discreetly behind a walled garden area. The half-hexagon cut-out in the bagged brick garden wall is signature Taglietti. What is visible from the street makes a strong statement, and Taglietti's philosophy is at

work here. He talks of the 'plane of the earth' which follows the land; the 'vertical plane' is subject to gravitational forces, and this he tries to break visually by use of strong shadow or, in other instances, windows that are not quite vertical. The third and, to his mind, 'freest' of the planes is the 'roof plane' and throughout his career Taglietti's roof lines, which have in his words 'the greatest possibility for shaping an architectural space', are a signature feature of his work.

Here, in the Dingle House, it is the various horizontal roof planes which define the exterior space. A public building Taglietti was working on in the same period, the Associated Chamber of Manufacturers Conference Centre, employs the same timber fascia with angled edges and overlapping roof lines to cap the main structure. While the fascia are finer in this domestic setting, they are more complex in their arrangement and impart a strong sense of form. They offset the solidity of the vertical planes and create a certain dynamism through the exaggerated timber horizontals. Originally the house was bagged brick, painted white, with redwood timber used to create a strong contrast. This illustrates something of the sculptural, graphic qualities to which Taglietti was naturally inclined.

The house is not large, but the arrangement of the space is a clear interpretation of the needs of the client. In response to the site, the design solution is an ingenious three-way split level plan.

The entrance is via a walled garden and leads directly into the dining room and kitchen level. These two rooms are connected by a large serving hatch in the

wall dividing them and an open corridor which runs straight from the front door to the rear of this platform, where the master bedroom and bathroom are located.

The living area, with study at the north end, runs the length of the house, and is accessed by a small set of stairs at each end of the entry level corridor. (Stairs at the far end of the corridor lead down to a children's bedroom, guest bedroom and bathroom.)

The living space benefits from a high ceiling with clerestory windows running the western length of the room. Hence privacy is maintained but light is admitted. This extra height is clad in redwood timber which adds warmth to the space. Also connecting the split-level living spaces, by spanning the lower and upper level, is a brick column, bagged and painted, which forms the fireplace. Located centrally in the living room, it also features an open area for wood storage. The overall effect is of a continuous interconnected space, yet each with a specific function. The dining area is visible from the living area, while the kitchen is connected to both the living and dining areas. The generous deck, which faces north towards the garden and golf course, and wraps around the building to the east, is accessed directly via floor-to-ceiling glass doors from the living area. The play of intersecting volumes creates an open and fluid scheme that makes the most of the site and the available space, and clearly connects inside with out.

Decoratively, the spaces are simple. The long, slim windows and timber cladding give a measured, linear feel to the house. The colour scheme of white

The open plan living space is divided by
a painted brick fireplace. A large cavity in
the structure is a storage area for wood.
To the right is a second set of stairs, this
time linking with the kitchen so that the
flow between the two levels is continuous.

painted walls and wood detailing is rather like the original exterior, showing the visible connection between the two. The kitchen and bedroom cupboards reflect this aesthetic. White melamine faced and with a deep wood trim, they are designed without the interruption of handles.

As Andrew Metcalf points out in his book *Canberra Houses*, the Dingle House is an example of 'Taglietti's dual theme of sheltering privacy externally and spatial finery internally'. In fact, this level of privacy in terms of creating an almost fortress-like façade to the street was taken to new levels in the Paterson House (1968) and the Evan House (1971) where the life of the house, complete with internal courtyards, took place inside the enclosure. While the Dingle House is less extreme, it illustrates many of Taglietti's architectural ideas – the play of volumes, the sense of unfolding internal spaces, the freedom expressed by the roof line and the ability to work with the site to find the optimum outcome.

OPPOSITE: This was originally a study area at the rear of the living room, separated from the staircase by a low blade wall. THIS PAGE: The wall of glass allows the greenery to form part of the room's decor. Facing towards the Federal Golf Course, the deck is well placed for sunlight and view.

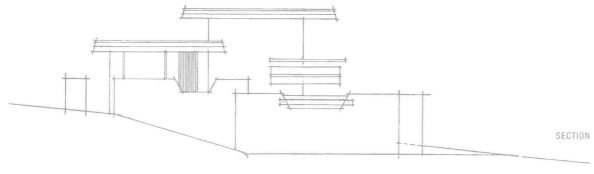

SECTION

DETAILS THE DINGLE HOUSE

COPPER LIGHT FITTING/TIMBER

Taglietti designed the square copper light shades that are dotted around the house. In this instance, the light is wall-mounted to illuminate the stairs from the dining room up to the living space. The copper material is sympathetic in colour to the wooden panelling that runs along the west side of the living area, interrupted only by a slice of window. The clean palette of white walls combined with timber floors gives the space a certain warmth and humanity. This long living/study space, which runs from the front of the house to the back, is broken up by the two blade walls at the side of the staircases and the rather monumental brick fireplace at the room's centre.

CLEMENT MEADMORE CHAIR

Clement Meadmore began his career designing furniture and lighting but after the success of his first solo sculpture show in 1953, he turned his attentions purely to that medium. The Cord chair, designed in 1952, was made from mild steel rods, welded together and painted black to form the frame. The seat and back are a type of sling design using cotton braid or cord. Later, the chairs were also offered with a synthetic braid. Melbourne manufacturer Michael Hirst produced a range of Meadmore-designed products, including a dining table and glass-topped coffee table. Taglietti knew Meadmore and had, in fact, commissioned him to create panels for a motel project he was working on.

KITCHEN
While the kitchen is compact, it is well designed and conveniently located. A large serving hatch (which originally had a fold-down bench on the reverse side) directly accesses the dining room, and the kitchen is also open to the main corridor. The stove, with its splashback of white ceramic tiles, has plenty of serving space adjacent to it. The generous drawers and cupboards are of white laminate with deep timber edge detailing. The design requires no handles and became something of a Tagliotti trademark. He favoured this treatment for wardrobes both in this house and others of a later period.

BAGGED BRICK WALL While Taglietti favoured the plasticity of working in concrete due to the immense flexibility of form it could deliver, the Dingle House is of brick cavity wall construction which was rendered and, originally, painted white. A means of breaking up the visual solidity of the wall is Taglietti's signature void – in this instance a half-hexagon shape seemingly cut out of the brickwork. Architecture, in Taglietti's view, 'should achieve being a piece of art', and his buildings all have a supremely sculptural quality. Much later, in 1978, Taglietti's celebrated War Memorial Repository in Canberra utilises a dynamic geometric opening in the walled building to great dramatic effect.

NOGUCHI LIGHT The 1N is one of the smaller lights from the vast range of Akari lights designed by Japanese-American Isamu Noguchi. In the 25-year period from 1951, Noguchi designed over 100 lights for traditional Japanese paper light manufacturer, Ozeki & Co in Gifu. Available in table, floor and pendant varieties, the shapes range from the geometric to the biomorphic. Each light is assembled in hand-made paper from mulberry bark known as mino-gami. This paper has a softness that diffuses light beautifully and is less fragile than the cheaper rice paper commonly used. The fine bamboo ribs are still wound by hand around the original wooden block moulds which were made to Noguchi's specification.

WINDOW Slim windows are used throughout the living space to admit light but maintain privacy. Not only is the vertical window (shown above) used, but horizontal clerestory windows also run along the west-facing wall in the living area, ensuring daylong light. Privacy was something Taglietti strove for in his houses and while this house does not quite turn its back to the street in the manner of some Sydney School houses of the period, it is certainly giving it the cold shoulder. Internally the house has an open-plan feel, albeit on different levels, and all the generosity of view is concentrated at the back where large glass doors face towards the golf course.

GRUZMAN WAS A PIONEER OF NEW
TECHNOLOGIES, AND MUCH OF
THE EFFECTIVENESS OF THIS HOUSE
COMES FROM THE MANNER IN WHICH
HE MANIPULATES SPACE THROUGH
THE USE OF MATERIALS.

PREVIOUS PAGES: Neville Gruzman's perfectly sited house, at the end of a cul-de-sac, with dramatic views over a gorge. Privacy was created by Gruzman's landscaping – a series of man-made hills on the approach to the house to screen it from view. The cantilevered platform is part of a major extension to the house in 1983, also by Gruzman. OPPOSITE: Gruzman was interested in new technologies and this pavilion in glass, timber and concrete illustrates some of his preoccupations. The house originally comprised a bedroom and bathroom mezzanine at entrance level and a large open-plan living area of double height, as shown, on the lower level.

'I REALLY DISLIKE GRUZMAN BECAUSE HE IS THE most aggravating, demanding, sometimes impossible person I have ever known – nothing is ever done well enough to satisfy him – he is concerned for reaching for the stars…the result is that he has given me two heart attacks, caused me to have a quadruple bypass and in the end will be the death of me.'

It was with these words that Neville Gruzman himself opened his talk (Gruzman on Gruzman) to the members of the Royal Australian Institute of Architects (RAIA). It was his way of acknowledging his reputation for being difficult to deal with; his way of letting *them* know that *he* knew.

This lecture, conducted entirely in the third person, explained something of his past. 'Gruzman grew up in the Depression – as a result he had a depressed personality – he will never throw anything away.' More poignantly, the stresses of the Depression are said to have killed his father, a Jewish immigrant, who, with Gruzman's mother, ran a pub in the Sydney suburb of Matraville. 'Gruzman's widowed mother set out to bring up her three sons on a tiny income, ensuring that they got love, affection and a good education,' he told his audience. However, he was later to acknowledge the lack of a male role model, and felt fortunate to have a series of significant influences which helped to fill this gap.

Neville and his brother Laurence converted to Anglicanism and went to Sydney Boys High School. Subsequently, his time at the University of Sydney was a mixed bag. 'I was a lousy student and I struggled through third year,' Gruzman once said. The acting dean went so far as to tell him he would never make it as an architect. With a typical spirit of defiance he thought,

'I'll show the bastard.' And then, what Gruzman describes as a miracle happened in the form of the Hungarian lecturer, cartoonist and architect George Molnar, who had arrived in Sydney fresh from the modern movement in Europe.

Up till then, the study of architectural history had concluded at the end of the nineteenth century and so, until Molnar's teaching, there had been no mention of the work of Le Corbusier or Mies van der Rohe. Molnar's Point Piper flat became a place for discussion, debate and the drinking of red wine. 'Molnar would settle in a chair he designed himself – set himself up like a little god – and espouse architectural philosophy,' Gruzman recalled. His eyes were further opened by his friend and contemporary, Bruce Rickard, who introduced him to the work of American architect Frank Lloyd Wright.

As a student, Gruzman also found pleasure in attending the freehand drawing classes of eminent artist Lloyd Rees. The tide in Gruzman's relationship with architecture was turning, and another piece of good fortune was to come his way. An aunt was creating a subdivision of waterfront land at Rose Bay and part of the condition of sale was that her nephew, the architecture student, was to design the house. He later admitted this was rather daring on her part. The resulting house, influenced by Le Corbusier, was such a success that the builder asked him to design a house for himself next door. Suddenly the student, who graduated in 1952 and was expected not to make it as an architect, had two waterfront homes to his name by his fourth year of study.

An epiphany of sorts occurred in Sydney's The Craftsman Bookshop in 1955.

He came across a book published the same year called *Architectural Beauty in Japan*, picturing the Ryoan-ji sand garden in Kyoto. So deeply felt was his reaction to what he saw that he promptly abandoned his practice and, at the Japanese government's invitation, moved to Japan for four-and-a-half months of study. The Ryoan-ji sand garden didn't disappoint. The effect of its beauty was 'transporting', and he saw clearly that 'architecture is more than putting together space and material; there are heights that we as creators can reach'. He praised the Katsura Imperial Villa for its spatial qualities, particularly the relationship of inner and outer space, and level of detailing.

Once he returned to Australia, Japanese architecture had an enormous impact on his work – the use of materials, the level of craftsmanship and the intellectual rigour all shaped Gruzman's sensibility. He went so far as to announce that post-Japan he was a 'born-again architect'.

Working on Sydney's North Shore in the 1950s and 1960s, he produced a number of houses that reflected his natural flamboyance. There's a theory that because his style was hard to pigeonhole, and he didn't adhere consistently to any particular school of architecture, he has received less recognition than he deserves. Gruzman himself was of the opinion that his buildings had no obvious signature, that each project was answered with its own set of architectural solutions dictated by the site and needs of the client.

Indeed, a snapshot of three houses built around the same time show his diversity. The Salz House, in Rose Street, Mosman (1960), uses unadorned clinker brick in a strict linear design recalling the work of Frank Lloyd Wright; the Holland House in Middle Cove

The bookshelf and wall cabinet are where the kitchen was once sited. The original cantilevered cabinet was in stainless steel and illustrates Gruzman's forward thinking in his early adoption of the open-plan, one-wall kitchen. The pair of Wassily chairs by Marcel Breuer, to the left, are where the dining table would have been situated. The mirrored pillar houses plumbing pipes and electrical cables and was originally glass fronted to expose the inner workings, and partially painted to form a 'vertical sculpture'.

The remarkable sculptural fireplace and stairway is the centrepiece of the room. Its gravity-defying structure illustrates something of the bravado that characterises Gruzman's architecture. This view is from the lower level of the dining area, through the stairs to the living space and out to the bush. Concrete was formed to make a platform for the sofas, which were originally covered in black and white ponyskin.

(1961) is a modernist cantilevered structure, predominantly built in glass and timber, and is restrained and geometric, while the Chadwick House in Forestville (1961–64) is an organic cave-like dwelling constructed of a series of interlocking hexagons using bush stone. Bruce Rickard, however, points to their similarities. 'They all have a beautiful spatial flow, the living areas all face north and they are exquisitely detailed.' Whatever the style, these buildings all have the panache of their creator; as Peter Watts, director of the Historic Houses Trust, said of the houses, they are 'one-off major gestures, very Hollywood glamour'.

Two aspects of Gruzman's architectural philosophy are outlined in *Australian Style*, a book written by Babette Hayes and April Hersey in 1970. The first is to do with siting for maximum sunlight. 'Even in the brief winter months the admission of the winter sun can do more than merely supplement other forms of heating…its sense of warmth can be developed by the architect when he encourages it to push deeply into the space to paint the interior with its pale golden light.' The second is to do with privacy, and he talks of 'that increasingly elusive quality of privacy, now almost lost to us, privacy visually and privacy audibly'.

The issue of privacy would have received a thorough exploration for Gruzman while designing the Rosenburg/Hills House on Sydney's upper North Shore. His bachelor client, Sam Rosenburg, was a practising naturist and wanted to be able to 'wander around his house nude', said Gruzman. Not something, one suspects, the rather conservative suburb of North Turramurra would approve of. Rosenburg had read a *Sydney Morning Herald* article by Gruzman on architectural education, and commissioned him to build his home on that basis alone.

The large site sits at the end of a cul-de-sac, overlooking a gorge. Gruzman, who had also studied landscape architecture, created a sense of arrival by designing impressive semi-circular walls at the entrance from the street and a long driveway curving down to the house. He built a series of hills which screen the approach to the house, and created a dramatic waterfall, the sound of which fills the air. This planned environment formed the perfect context for the house.

Gruzman was very attuned to the land he built on, and the setting for the Rosenburg/Hills House is incredibly dramatic; perfect for an architect whose work is described by Professor Philip Goad as 'theatrical and performative'. Overlooking this majestic bushland view, the house itself seems to settle with a light touch on the land. Constructed of glass, timber and concrete, it echoes rather than mimics a Japanese aesthetic. It also, as Goad points out, 'brought together two iconic twentieth century houses (Wright's Fallingwater, and Mies van der Rohe's Farnsworth House) to create the ultimate diagram of abstract shelter in the landscape'.

Gruzman was a pioneer of new technologies, and much of the effectiveness of this house comes from the manner in which he manipulates space through the use of materials. Walls of glass are intersected by a roof line which butts into the interior; double-height pillars give a monumental sense, and the central sculptural fireplace, integrated into the staircase, is engineered to appear to defy gravity. It is a house without a bad angle, inside or out; it is highly photogenic.

The front door is large and imposing for a house that is more like a large-scale pavilion. At entrance level is a bathroom and bedroom open to the amazing view. Downstairs is a large dining and living area. Three sides are glass, and the rear wall, which is solid, originally supported a cantilevered stainless steel bench which constituted the kitchen. Today, the one-wall kitchen, open to a larger room, is commonplace but in 1966 it was a radical way of approaching the lifestyle requirements of his client. It recalls one of Molnar's cartoons for *The Sydney Morning Herald*, showing two rather hoity-toity ladies with the caption, 'We don't eat in the kitchen, we cook in the dining room.'

It was Gruzman's view that 'outside spaces are often rightly regarded as extensions of inside spaces', and the concrete platform that extends from the living area faces north, guaranteeing daylong sunlight. The linking of indoor and outdoor space is strengthened by the use of concrete in both areas – a material that Gruzman felt was organic, and connected readily to the landscape.

When designed in 1966, it had a bold interior created by the famous Australian decorator, Marion Hall Best. The carpets were bright red, the sofas ponyskin, the mullions were painted dark crimson, and Marcel Breuer Cessna cantilevered chairs sat around the Eames Aluminium Group dining table. This avant-garde approach was also matched by Gruzman touches – a square, glass-faced pillar that housed the plumbing for the bathroom was originally painted various colours by Leonard Hessing to create, in Gruzman's words, 'a vertical sculpture'. This was a seriously cool, designer bachelor pad set amongst the gum trees.

The original owner only lived in the house for a few years before his death, and it fell into rather unsympathetic hands. Many of the attributes that made it great were either covered or corrupted. Besser blocks and beaten copper panels were a crude attempt to create privacy, and although the new owners sought Gruzman's advice, he didn't take up the challenge.

Thankfully, the next owners, Michael and Kerrie Hills, who bought in the early Eighties, appreciated the good bones beneath the vulgar add-ons. Not only did they set about restoring it but, with the needs of their growing family in mind, contacted Gruzman with a view to a substantial addition. Gruzman came to 'interview' the Hills in their rather conservative house in Sydney's Beecroft and agreed to take on the project. Later, at a pre-arranged meeting at the Turramurra house, he was more than an hour late. Upset by the neglect he was aware it had suffered over the years, he had forgotten its exact location and got lost.

Space had been left on the site for an addition and, in 1983, it was built, complete with a truly spectacular bathroom. As John Haskell in his article on Gruzman for *Art & Australia* points out, 'The house therefore combines Gruzman's work over almost 20 years and again shows his remarkable consistency of style.'

Part of the reason Gruzman produced such successful houses is attributed to his ability to connect with his clients, to take on not only their practical living demands but also their personal traits and attitudes and mould them into a very personal building. The Hills had a long and pleasurable relationship with Gruzman. 'He was always generous with his time and would discuss the most minute details with us, sometimes over hours,' says Michael Hills. He acknowledges frustrations but senses that Gruzman, having regretted compromising in the past, simply didn't want to do it anymore. In his quest for perfection, cost was never an issue. As Kerrie Hills astutely points out, 'Neville needed patrons, not clients.' But the Hills do credit Gruzman with opening their eyes to a different way of seeing things. 'He was opinionated but always spent the time to talk it through,' says Michael Hills. 'He was widely read and extremely knowledgeable. He got us young and made us part of the process.'

In Gruzman's own Darling Point home, glamour played a central role. The bathroom alone speaks volumes. A completely mirrored space, it allows for endless, faceted reflections – leading more than one journalist to draw the analogy between it and the multi-faceted nature of Gruzman's personality. As well as an

architect, he was for many years the very vocal Mayor of Woollahra, in Sydney's eastern suburbs, and a dedicated university lecturer, giving generously of his time to students, beyond the call of duty.

Conversely, he was a highly successful litigant and in almost 50 years had taken 30 cases to court. This is only matched by the staggering number of times the accident-prone Gruzman was admitted to Sydney's St Vincent's Hospital – 40 times in 30 years.

Over the years, the written word became increasingly important to him and, holding fast to the view that 'architects have a responsibility to the built and natural environment', nothing much escaped his eagle eye. The standards he set for himself he also expected of others, and more than once was reprimanded by the RAIA for the public criticism of the work of fellow architects.

His personal life appears highly charged and passionate and yet in his work he found inspiration in the principles of Japanese architecture, striving to create serene buildings that harmonise with their surroundings. As Professor Philip Goad said, 'His work, like his personality, was chimerical, brilliant, outspoken and assertive. You could not divorce the two.' Through a lack of compromise comes a reputation for being difficult. Through lack of compromise also come great buildings.

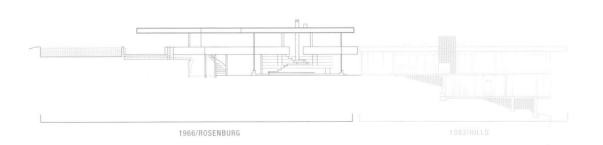

1966/ROSENBURG   1983/HILLS

The concrete used internally is extended out to form a north-facing platform. Gruzman considered concrete an organic material which connected with the landscape. It is also an extension of his philosophy of relating the house to the land, and siting for maximum sunlight.

DETAILS THE ROSENBURG/HILLS HOUSE

STAIRCASE Gruzman's passion for Japanese architecture did not limit his concepts to the handcrafted or low-tech. Instead, he embraced the principles and married them with his own interests in engineering and with technological advances in the use of glass, steel and concrete. The integrated staircase and fireplace in the Rosenburg/Hills House is a case in point. Here, Gruzman has combined functionality with a dramatic sculptural centrepiece. An engineer friend who had worked on Centrepoint Tower in Sydney's CBD visited the house, looked at the staircase and said, 'What's holding that up?' The very open hearth gives the sense of a campfire in the way the wood is arranged and adds an elemental touch to a very sophisticated interior.

WATERFALL Gruzman's idea for this house was to maximise privacy. Visually this was achieved by the man-made hills (the client acquired earth from local roadworks) which were constructed along the approach to the house from the street, with some being up to 10 metres high. Gruzman was also sensitive to 'privacy audibly', and the inclusion of a waterfall within the grounds creates a completely secluded environment where nature can be seen and heard. At night the bushland animals, including possums, wallabies and large goannas, wander onto the concrete platform.

FURNISHINGS Within his glass pavilion, Gruzman was anxious to give his client a sense of enclosure. One of the ways he did this was with the symmetrical placement of the sofas on the formed concrete platform. The platform doubles as a step-up to the doors, again illustrating Gruzman's virtuosity in streamlining the functional needs of a space. Originally, as part of interior decorator Marion Hall Best's scheme, the sofas were covered in ponyskin, and the floor covered in a bright red shag pile carpet. The contrast with the raw concrete was bold but very effective. The ponyskin sofas have been replaced with Antonio Citterio Diesis sofas customised to fit on the concrete slab.

DOORS The elegantly proportioned floor-to-ceiling glass doors open onto the north-east facing cantilevered concrete platform. The doors, with their fine window mullions and predominance of glass, create a minimal barrier between the interior and exterior, and the consistent use of concrete makes the transition seamless from one to the other. Gruzman was passionate about sensitive siting to maximise sunlight, which was particularly important in this case, with the client being a naturist.

EXTERIOR LIGHTING Gruzman's words best describe his approach to the exterior lighting scheme. 'I always use lighting in gardens so that at night they almost become part of the interior space. In this project I did something quite different. By concealed lighting around all of the edges of the roofs, I actually provided almost all of the internal lighting by reflecting it from outside to inside through the glass walls. The effect of this was at night to allow the occupants to live in a large pool of light that [combined] inside and outside as one.' By day, siting makes the most of natural light, while by night the lighting scheme is another device to unify interior and exterior.

MIES VAN DER ROHE MR40 The MR40 by Mies van der Rohe was one of a line of metal framed cantilevered chair designs that he worked on from 1926–31. This particular model was a reworking of the earlier MR20 chair which was manufactured by Thonet with either a textile or a woven cane seat. The MR40 added luxurious rolls of padded leather to an already extremely comfortable design. 'You will be sitting on a column of air,' the Bauhaus catalogues boasted of the cantilevered concept. Contemporaneous to Mies van der Rohe's experimentation with tubular metal cantilevered chairs, Marcel Breuer, Mart Stam, Hans Luckhardt and Anton Lorenz were producing their own versions. The chair has been produced by Knoll International since 1953.

BRUCE RICKARD'S APPROACH TO
ARCHITECTURE IS HUMAN IN BOTH
ITS SCALE AND ITS SENSITIVITY.
IT IS ESSENTIALLY LIFE AFFIRMING,
OPTIMISTIC AND MAKES A MEANINGFUL
CONNECTION WITH NATURE.

PREVIOUS PAGES: Set on a battleaxe block amongst angophoras, the Bruce Rickard house sits into the hillside. Built in sandstock brick and timber, it blends seamlessly with the landscape. An original light detail in the living area. OPPOSITE: Rickard places great emphasis on the connection between indoor and outdoor spaces. Hence floor-to-ceiling timber-framed doors open up to allow the integration of the two. The Heart chair and table by Danish furniture designer Hans Wegner continue the feeling of wood and warmth.

By using the same sandstock bricks for the internal and external walls, and continuing the treatment of the western red cedar ceiling to the underside of the eaves, the sense of continuous space is emphasised. The courtyard faces north to capture as much sunlight as possible.

I HAVE TO COME CLEAN AND CONFESS THAT I am a fan of Bruce Rickard's work in general and this house in particular. For seven years it has been home to my family, and so my experience of Rickard's architecture is a very personal one. I can still recall when a colleague showed me snaps of the Marshall House which was for sale for the first time since it was built in 1967. Its special qualities were immediately evident, and I have to say, still are.

Born in 1929, Rickard studied architecture at Sydney Technical College in the evenings while working during the day for celebrated architect Sydney Ancher. In 1954 he travelled to the UK where he studied landscape architecture at University College London, and in 1956 received a fellowship to study at the University of Pennsylvania, Philadelphia. In Europe and America Rickard had the opportunity to see the work of many of the great modernists of the day, such as Le Corbusier and Mies van der Rohe, but it was the houses of Frank Lloyd Wright that he 'found staggering'. He admired the way they responded to the site, the flowing spaces and the warm feeling, 'like the inside of a rum barrel'. He saw a lot of Wright's work during his time there, and was convinced that architecturally this was the way forward. Coming home to Australia in 1959, he was free to adapt Wrightian principles to the local climate and culture, and create from it his own distinctive signature style.

Bruce Rickard was 36 and already had 26 domestic residences under his belt when Penny and Greg Marshall approached him on the recommendation of their friend Richard Leplastrier, an architecture student at the time.

By this time Rickard had already worked through many of the principles that have endured throughout his long career. The house he built in 1961 in Kokoda Avenue, Wahroonga, for his own family and architectural practice, was something of a model for the Marshall House. There's the strong emphasis on living spaces – indoor and out – and the flow between the two; the choice of natural, organic materials, and the desire to add warmth with as much winter sun as possible through sensitive siting. Both projects tackled the difficulties of building on a battleaxe block. Rickard, surprisingly, expresses a preference for this narrow type of block as it 'allows you [the architect] to extend your wings'.

Articulating the philosophy that has informed his architecture throughout his working life, Rickard, in 1994, described buildings 'that allow and encourage people in their everyday life to enjoy and partake of the pleasant sensations emanating from climate and the natural and built environment, such as the wellbeing felt from sun in winter and shade in summer; the delight of seeing trees, plants and the sky'. Before I read this, I implicitly knew it to be true. There are those moments in life which one doesn't often appreciate are the result of someone else's consideration – the ability to read the Saturday paper in winter in a patch of sunlight; coming up the stairs each morning to a knockout view framed by trees; taking a coffee in a sun-dappled courtyard as the children potter around. Rickard's approach to architecture is human in both its scale and sensitivity. It is essentially life affirming, optimistic and makes a meaningful connection with nature.

The Marshall House was built on a rather restrictive block – down a steep driveway with a sewer line running through the west of it. For this reason the top of the block was chosen, which also had the advantage of securing better views. The house is a typical example of Rickard's ability to extend the living space by blurring the line between inside and out. 'One of the design problems was where to put the front door,' says Rickard. 'The terrace, facing north, was the best spot for the outdoor living area but as it also had a view, a front door would have blocked all that out.' In the end, the idea of a conventional front door was abandoned and, instead, a bank of glass and timber doors, all opening outwards to the courtyard, serve to give the house a broad and welcoming aspect. On the south side, a deck captures the view across the Spit Bridge and beyond.

The main living space is one large room flanked by the two outdoor spaces. As with some of Rickard's other buildings, it pivots around the central core of a fireplace on one side and galley kitchen on the other. The fireplace is generous and open, with a hob for a tray to its left, used as a seat by both us and the Marshalls. The kitchen is a simple design of great ingenuity. Not only has it endured 40 years of use with immense durability, but its stylistic devices are still the source of admiration. A stainless steel bench runs the length of it, behind which is a recessed cupboard housing everything from recipe books to condiments. Three extra chopping boards, or pot stands, slide out from under the benchtops and long thin timber

THIS PAGE: A Hans Wegner CH24 sits in front of built-in kitchen units and shelving. Fluorescent lighting is discreetly hidden under the top strip of wood to illuminate the working surfaces. OPPOSITE: The simple galley kitchen has a stainless steel bench on one side (just visible to the left) and a row of cupboards on the other. Simply and inexpensively designed, it has endured 40 years of use without addition or amendment.

ABOVE: The fireplace is set within the sandstock brick core of the living space (the kitchen is located behind it). To avoid the appearance of a flat wall, interest is created by the play of planes formed by the bricks. There is a hob to the left of the fire for a tray or a cushion. OPPOSITE: The line of the roof is cantilevered, which emphasises the low, horizontal design.

shelves are perfect for having everyday cooking ingredients to hand.

The cupboards are all in laminated timber with brass D-handles. The style has lasted because it is simple. It was also economical. The Marshalls would be the first to admit that the house had to be built within a strict budget and that they entrusted the project entirely to Rickard without much interference, enabling the architect's vision to remain intact.

The living area faces west and, while the view is compelling, Rickard chose to build a solid wall along its length to absorb the heat of the westerly afternoon sun. The view is revealed by a large window to the left of this wall, and glass doors lead out onto the deck. What works so well about this design is its ability to adapt to seasonal change. In summer, all the doors can be opened up, extending the living areas out onto the deck and courtyard. In winter, the house closes down, the solid wall creating a sense of protection against the elements, while the centrally placed fireplace provides a source of heat and comfort.

The lower floor houses three bedrooms and a workroom, originally used for carpentry projects, but now a study. The bedrooms, as Rickard says, are like 'ship's cabins', but all have double-glass doors onto the west-facing deck to allay any sense of being closed in. Everything is built in, so the only additional items required are a bed and chair. The rooms have laminated timber built-in cupboards, a simple desk and a shelf that sits over the bedhead, and houses two light bulbs. The bedrooms are a pleasing mix of brick, cedar panelling, and white painted plasterboard. Both bathrooms (one ensuite) are small and serviceable but far

THIS PAGE: The bedrooms, which Rickard describes as 'cabin-like', retain a feeling of spaciousness as they all open onto the lower deck. OPPOSITE: The bedrooms have a simple shelf with hidden reading lights above the bed. The considerate detailing reduces the need for too much extraneous decoration.

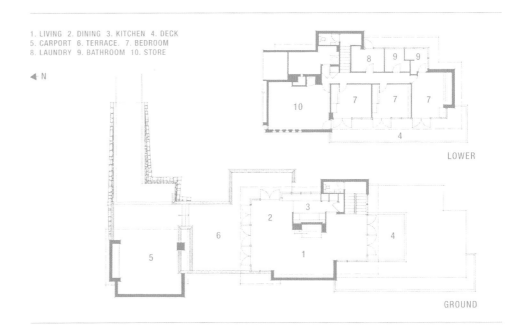

1. LIVING 2. DINING 3. KITCHEN 4. DECK
5. CARPORT 6. TERRACE. 7. BEDROOM
8. LAUNDRY 9. BATHROOM 10. STORE

◀ N

LOWER

GROUND

Each bedroom has a built-in desk. In the master bedroom, the wide western red cedar boards are visually extended by the mirror on the rear wall. An original Cherner chair sits in front of the desk. The high set windows show how Rickard butted glass edges together for a seamless effect.

from the luxury of today's bathroom requirements, and have had the original bronze/brown glass mosaics replaced with sturdier slate tiles.

Much of the house's warmth comes from the choice of materials. The construction material is predominantly recycled sandstock bricks sourced from Paddington houses demolished when the Eastern Suburbs Railway was being built. They are undeniably bricks of character. Small explosions of impurities in the clay add bursts of grey to the soft sand base colour. Bricks are used both externally and internally and are left unadorned. The brick is combined with shiplapped western red cedar chosen for its richness and depth, and used for all windows and doors. This timber was even used for the living room ceiling, and the choice of wide boards running the length of the space creates a linear pattern that elongates the room.

One of the fundamental, but often neglected, aspects of a home is the choice of lighting. I have grown up with a central ceiling light and a lamp. Here, the lighting plan is ingenious but, in keeping with the house, modest. In the bedrooms, the main switch turns on recessed lights above the wardrobe doors. Upstairs, set into the red cedar ceiling are six recessed lights 20 cm square; discreetly hidden behind a timber strip in the kitchen are long fluorescent tubes, and built into the shelving that runs the length of the living area are lights behind specially constructed shades in linen-covered Perspex. The combination of different lights allows for infinite variety and the ability to 'close down' certain areas at night to create a feeling of intimacy while eating, reading or just watching TV.

As for the landscaping, Penny Marshall tells how it was Rickard who introduced

her to native plants. He had studied landscape design, and in Pennsylvania had been impressed by an exhibition of the work of Burle Marx, who used natives. Returning home, Rickard found it hard to find Australian natives – nurseries had few, and officials for public planning favoured British plants. Around Lake Burley Griffin, for example, they wanted weeping willows, not river red gums.

The Marshalls opted to plant natives and the house is now surrounded by huge angophoras and native flowering plants which in turn attract birds. The setting is complete. After 33 years, the Marshalls sold their house to us and commissioned Rickard to design a second house for them. Looking through his lifelong list of projects it is interesting just how many clients have come back for a second house...and then there are those who have simply never left.

DETAILS THE MARSHALL HOUSE

BUILT-IN LIGHT In Bruce Rickard houses of this period, the lighting scheme was comprehensively considered. Here, the light fitting has been combined with a shelving unit which runs the entire length of the west-facing brick wall in the living room. 40 mm meranti (Pacific maple) timber sandwiches a light shade, custom-made for the purpose. Linen was wrapped around Perspex to form a rectangular shade while the light bulb and switch were discreetly tucked away from sight. The combination of materials shown here illustrates something of Rickard's preference for honest, unadorned materials – brick, timber and linen – that require no enhancement and stand the test of time.

TIMBER PANELLING Whereas upstairs on the living/dining level, brick is the predominant material, it plays a smaller role in the bedroom area. Shiplap panelling, laminated timber and white-painted plasterboard are also used in the materials mix. 23 cm-wide boards in western red cedar wrap around the stairwell wall and are held in place with exposed copper nails. The rich colour and grain of the wood imparts the warmth that Rickard strove for in his architecture. Set into the timber is a recessed timber-framed light which can be switched on and off at either the top or bottom of the stairs. All the switches are placed at a very low level, making them easy for children to use.

POT STANDS The galley kitchen is streamlined and functional with plenty of cupboards and shelves but not an enormous amount of preparation space. Integrated into the design of the kitchen cabinetry are three pull-out pot stands or chopping boards, which are constantly in use. They significantly increase the sense of useable space but can be put away equally easily. The simple brass D-handles used throughout the kitchen are completely in tune with the unpretentious quality of the design.

SHELVING While Rickard didn't design the furniture for his houses, he did design many elements of the interior, greatly reducing the need for extraneous pieces of furniture or lighting. His solutions were often simple and economical. For example, each of the bedrooms has a slim shelf above the bed. The surface is useful for books and ornaments but, at two points underneath, are light bulbs and a switch, forming an integrated reading light. There is also a light to illuminate the wardrobes, illustrating Rickard's preference for localised lighting sources rather than the general glare of a central light.

RECESSED STORAGE The galley kitchen bench is one piece of formed stainless steel with an integrated double sink in the centre. While it has lost its shine over the years, it has gained the patina of a matt, much-used surface that continues to look good despite 40 years of service. A long cupboard with sliding plywood doors is recessed behind this bench, and houses cookery books at one end, condiments in the middle and large serving bowls at the other. It means functional items can be hidden from view yet easily accessed. The base of this cupboard is also stainless steel, making it easy to maintain. The cupboards above continue to ceiling level, maximising storage in what is essentially a small space.

OUTDOOR ROOM At the south side of the living room is a deck surrounded by trees on two sides and facing the Spit Bridge on the other. The shiplapped western red cedar balustrade gives a sense of enclosure and echoes the timber treatment internally. All the doors from the living room are floor-to-ceiling height and disappear when open, thus increasing the sense that the deck is an extension of the living space – in essence, an outdoor room. As the deck is exposed to very strong westerly sun, the untreated hardwood timber on the floor has weathered to a silvery grey.

THE DOMINANT FEATURE IS THE INCREDIBLE WAVE CEILING WHICH GIVES AN ORGANIC, EXPRESSIONIST FEEL TO THE ROOM. CEDAR BOARDS WERE STEAMED TO MAKE THEM PLIABLE, AND THEN BUHRICH NAILED EACH ONE INTO PLACE.

PREVIOUS PAGES: The Buhrich House is set on the water at the edge at Sydney's Sugarloaf Point and is approached from the road through low-lying bush. The unique blend of its design elements is immediately evident: the wave roof line, the organic use of concrete and the panel of threaded timber all creating the façade of this extraordinary house.
OPPOSITE: The open-plan living and dining space incorporates built-in elements which Buhrich designed himself: the sofa, dining table and storage cupboard, with ponyskin-covered chairs inspired by the Breuer Long Chair.

THERE ARE SOME HOUSES THAT JUST STAY with you. They capture your imagination the first time you see them and they live in the back of your mind forever.

In the Nineties, I was a devotee of British *Elle Decoration*, edited by the inspiring Ilse Crawford. Each month would deliver a mix of British and overseas stories that satisfied my growing appreciation of architecture and interiors. One memorable issue, in 1998, showcased the Buhrich House II in Sydney's Castlecrag. Architecturally there was a lot to absorb: the undulating wave roof line, the fire-engine red bathroom and the awe-inspiring setting. When I pictured this book on Australian modernist architecture in my mind's eye, this was one of the houses that defined it.

It was therefore with a sense of genuine excitement and curiosity that I made my way along Castlecrag's Edinburgh Road in search of number 375. The road is wide and impressive and has a broad range of architecturally interesting houses, such as Peter Muller's Audette House and fine examples of Walter Burley Griffin's work. At one stage, the road narrows to a lane and I think I have run out of numbers when, at the very end, at the very tip of Sugarloaf Point, there are some stone steps cutting through a low bush garden. And there, as described by architect Peter Myers, sits 'easily the best modern house in Australia'.

Architect Hugh Buhrich's path to this, his final destination, had been far from straightforward. Born in Hamburg in 1911, he had a difficult and disadvantaged childhood, made no easier by the suicide of his father on returning from the Russian front after the First World War. Buhrich is on record as being rather disparaging about the quality of his education, describing the Munich architectural school he attended as 'not very good' and completing his degree at 'a really shocking university'. On a more positive note, he worked in Berlin for Hans Poelzig, a prestigious architect with an enormous breadth of work, from the Poelzig Building at the Goethe University (1931) to large-scale set designs for film, including the 1925 production of *The Golem*. Fortuitously, also studying under Poelzig was Buhrich's wife-to-be, Eva. The circumstances leading up to the war pushed the couple around Europe – to Holland and then briefly to London where they were married, finally arriving on Australian shores in 1939. After a short-lived, shared architectural appointment in Canberra, war broke out and Buhrich joined the army. His son Neil recalls his father's time as a private in the Citizen Military Force (1942–45). Not trusted with real weaponry and trained with a wooden gun, he did, during games of chess and soccer, make lifelong contacts with fellow émigrés, who later provided the lion's share of his architectural commissions. Educated central Europeans, many Jewish, went on to become successful, and turned to their architect friend when any kind of building was required.

After the war, Eva embarked on a long writing and editing career that included architectural criticism, under her own name and several male pseudonyms, for *House & Garden* magazine. Eventually she wrote a column for *The Sydney Morning Herald*. Her writing work provided financial support, and her outgoing personality enabled the couple

Behind the timber textured wall is a concrete panel which appears to float in its glass surround. The waved roof line and ceiling add to the sensuous quality of the house.

OPPOSITE: The view from the living room.
THIS PAGE: The dining table is positioned on a raised area with the kitchen adjacent, accessed to the right of the table behind the bank of cabinets. The wallhanging is a piece of carpet customised by Buhrich to soften the appearance of the suspended concrete panel behind it.

The compact kitchen with its simple bank of built-in cupboards is enhanced by the beauty of the wave ceiling and the natural light it allows into the room.

to have an interesting social life that included artists Robert Klippel and Francis Lymburner. The Buhrichs also hosted discussion groups attended by immigrants intent on continuing the cultural life they had left behind in Europe.

What must have been a great disappointment to Buhrich was the refusal of the Board of Architects to recognise his qualifications and, in doing so, denying him the right to practise officially as an architect. 'The Buhrichs must have been somewhat nonplussed by the refusal, especially as the equivalent body in the UK, the RIBA, had clearly recognised them as a talented couple, and helped support them financially to make the trip to Australia,' comments Peter Myers. For many years Buhrich worked under the title of 'planning consultant' and much of his work was restricted to alterations and interiors. Neil Buhrich recalls his father sitting for the exams and while he passed on the technical specifications part of the test, it was the design component that caused his rejection. His ideas were perhaps too radical for the conservative mindset of the Board of Architects in the 1950s. In 1971, it gave him the acknowledgement that would have been so useful earlier in his working life. As a result, apart from a few synagogues, small business premises and car parks, there are no major public works to speak of.

He did, however, design around 20 domestic projects, many of which are now altered beyond recognition or demolished, but it is the house he built for himself, and pretty much by himself, between 1968 and 1972, that has become the enduring testimony to Buhrich's creative genius.

This 'intensely personal' project took four years to complete because most of the work – the hand cutting of sandstone, steaming and shaping of cedar for the ceiling, and designing specific pieces of furniture – was undertaken by himself and his assistant, Bill Chambers. There is a strong sense of a complete vision both externally and internally.

The house is built as an extension to an old Walter Burley Griffin structure which had been used as a fisherman's cottage and was bought with money received as reparations from Germany. Set on a difficult site with an incredible view, Buhrich's house settles into the landscape with a lightness that is both subtle and unassuming for such a remarkable building.

Buhrich was 57 when he designed this house, so it was to some degree the culmination of his ideas and influences. He had been a long-time admirer of the work of Ernest Plischke, an Austrian émigré who, like Buhrich, had fled Europe. He set up a practice in New Zealand and was also refused registration with the local architectural body, but was fortunate with his patronage and built some interesting houses. Thoroughly steeped in European culture, Plischke considered 'the aim to be to achieve a synthesis of the conception of space and sculptural quality. Each of these two components must be evolved out of the function and the construction of a building.' Although Buhrich was much more plain speaking and would not have chosen these words to express his vision, this philosophy is embodied in the Buhrich House II.

The last interview Hugh Buhrich gave before he died was with architectural critic Elizabeth Farrelly, for *Architecture Australia*. In it he explained in plain and practical terms how many of the sculptural elements, particularly the roof and ceiling, came about, and, indeed, they were the result of 'function and construction'. But there is too much ingenuity and beauty for one to be the mere result of another. The main living space is large and open, 10 metres by 7 metres. One wall of glass faces north-east, to the impressive view across Middle Harbour. The interior palette is natural – a mix of smooth black slate flooring, silver ash veneer for cupboards, hand cut local sandstone for the wall that houses the fireplace, cedar boards for the ceiling, and concrete for the wall. There is nothing special in this combination in itself; it is how it is used that makes it extraordinary.

The dominant feature is the incredible wave ceiling which gives an organic, expressionist feel to the room. Cedar boards were steamed to make them pliable, and then Buhrich nailed each one into place. They have stood the test of time remarkably well. Facing the bush is a 'floating' concrete wall inset with slim steel columns to provide support. The concrete wall is partially obscured inside by a carpet customised by Buhrich with a dark red wave pattern running through it – a subtle echo of the ceiling above.

Years of designing furniture for clients enabled Buhrich to integrate most of the furniture needs of the house into the overall plan. Very few extra items were needed and so the interior retains a completely resolved feel. The dining table sits on the slightly raised back platform of the living area. Its simple structure of a

THIS PAGE: The study area faces the view and shows another of Buhrich's furniture designs — the built-in desk. He favoured the Eames-designed chair, the DCM, in the dining area and also here at the desk. OPPOSITE: Wood panelling creates a corner for a double bed; the door leads directly to the bathroom.

metal bar with acrylic ribs supporting the smoked glass top gives the appearance of being barely there. Where the table meets the rough sandstone wall there is a picture window, precisely the same width, which serves to extend the eye-line along the table's surface to the bush outside.

The kitchen, accessed by the raised dining area, is compact but open to the larger living space. A bank of 15 press-open cupboards in silver ash veneer provides the divide between the kitchen and living space in a functional but sculptural way. More sculptural than functional, however, is the external staircase. Precast in concrete, it extends from a narrow deck outside the living area to the level below. Neil Buhrich points to his father's dislike of bureaucracy and there is something rather rebellious about this precarious twisting, turning, open-to-the elements staircase.

One of the most remarkable aspects of this already remarkable house is the bathroom. Nothing quite prepares you for it. Lulled by warm, organic shapes and natural tones, the fire-engine red bathroom in seamless fibreglass takes you completely by surprise. Again, Elizabeth Farrelly's article quotes Buhrich's practical view of its genesis. He had been boat building in fibreglass and was familiar with its properties. He didn't like fussy bathrooms but did like occasional strong colour. He presents it casually as though there was no other conceivable outcome of this set of parameters. With a large, uncurtained window to the view, nature is part of the decor and this combination of the highly man-made within a natural context somehow makes it all the more effective.

Buhrich has described this house as his 'most intensely personal' project and it hopefully would have gratified him to learn that in March 2006 it was named 'Building of the Decade' for the 1970s by a panel of RAIA judges. The architect refused registration all those years ago had designed a building which not only garnered much international acclaim (French critic Françoise Fromonot described it 'a truly radical building'), but has now been embraced as one of Australia's most defining domestic residences.

The bright red fibreglass bathroom is something of a tour de force in a house of natural toned materials. The floor-to-ceiling windows ensure that the view – the trees and the water – creates a natural element in this extraordinary man-made space.

1. ENTRY 2. LIVING 3. DINING 4. KITCHEN
5. STUDY 6. BEDROOM 7. BATHROOM 8. DECK

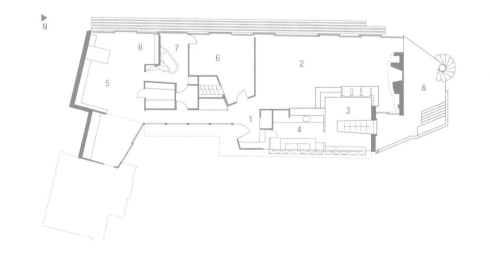

WINDOW AND TABLE Every element of the house was designed, created and crafted by Buhrich himself. This corner of the dining room encompasses many of the home's features. The rough-hewn sandstone wall gives an organic feel, but is broken by the precision of the window. The glass table top, supported by acrylic ribs that almost disappear, allows the eye to skim along the table to the window and enjoy a framed view of the bush beyond. The wallhanging, which looks like an artwork is, in fact, a piece of carpet that Buhrich himself customised to soften the appearance of the concrete panel when looking from inside out.

MATERIALS The Buhrich House uses a mix of materials in a highly inventive way which creates textural interest inside and out. This exterior wall is designed to disguise the concrete slab, and its threaded timbers imbue the building with a handcrafted feel. There is a balance at play of the natural and the artificial. The precision of the glass dining table contrasts with the handcut stone wall, while the fibreglass bathroom, the steamed cedar ceiling, the precast concrete and the customised wallhanging play with a variety of materials. Interestingly, they were all the product of Buhrich's creative sensibility, and it is to his great credit that these seemingly disparate materials hang together in such a cohesive and compelling fashion.

RED BATHROOM The bright red bathroom is an unexpected shot of exuberance in a house of earthy materials and natural colours. The use of fibreglass was a result of Buhrich's experience with boat building. The plasticity of the material allows for shapes to be moulded, and permits everything, from the shower and the soapdish to the bath and basin, to be integrated into a seamless design. The floor-to-ceiling windows with the treetop and water views mean the room is open to the elements, emphasising the contrast of man-made shapes and bold colour with the nature beyond.

KITCHEN The kitchen is incredibly small by today's standards and was tucked away between the storage cabinet shown (above right) and the back wall of the house. The windows under the undulating ceiling ensured it was light, but the compact nature of the space meant that everything had to have its place in order to operate efficiently. For example, the pots and pot lids were stored on the wall on small wooden pegs that acted as hooks or props. Sliding timber veneer doors and built-in kitchen cabinets gave the small space an integrated feel that blended into the overall scheme.

CEILING Many of Buhrich's architectural solutions were, he claimed, the result of a range of practical considerations. The wave ceiling came about while working through a strict set of building height regulations. In Buhrich's own words: 'It was just a practical response: I decided to push the ceiling up between the trusses.' The result is increased northerly light and, almost incidentally, an incredible expressionistic undulating ceiling. Inbuilt cabinetry, sofa and dining table ensured that the space needed little additional furniture. The fifteen-section cabinet (shown above) is in itself sculptural and divides the kitchen from the living area.

STAIRCASE While the Buhrich house is located in a bush setting on a spectacular piece of waterfront land, the interior and exterior are not connected in the way many of Buhrich's contemporaries sought to link the two spaces. Outside the floor-to-ceiling windows in the living room is a narrow balcony made of planks, purely for the practical purpose of cleaning the windows, and the access from this space to the floor below is via a daringly constructed external staircase. Precast concrete sections were configured in a dynamic spiral which, due to the lack of a handrail, creates a sense of adventure when descending it.

THE INTENTION WAS TO CREATE A
BUILDING THAT SAT LIGHTLY UPON THE
LAND. AS A RESULT, MANY OF THE
DESCRIPTIONS OF THE HOUSE LIKEN IT TO A
TENT, A NEST OR EVEN A GIANT SEABIRD.

PREVIOUS PAGES: Blending into the silvery greys of the surrounding bush setting is the holiday house of celebrated Australian photographer David Moore. Designed by architect Ian McKay after several false starts, the outcome has been described as 'a thoroughly modern masterpiece'. The tonal palette for the house is partly inspired by the much admired angophoras. OPPOSITE: Ian McKay acknowledges the dual influences of Australian vernacular and Japanese architecture. Hence the ability to mix a corrugated material for the roof with the sliding timber screens that divide the living area from the deck. From this outdoor extension of the living space there are stunning 180 degree views over Brisbane Water.

'THE HOUSE IS A SMALL CATHEDRAL OF TIMBER that caresses the trees' is the poetic description given by photographer David Moore of his Ian McKay-designed holiday house. But then the site itself, on the New South Wales Central Coast, was considered awe-inspiring. 'One of the most beautiful sites I have ever approached,' acknowledges McKay. Set high above the bay, on the edge of Bouddi National Park and overlooking Brisbane Water, the land is a tangle of mature angophoras and in Moore's words, 'lichen-covered rocks as big as houses'. Moore had acquired the land in 1968. He was recently divorced and wanted a weekender within reasonable striking distance of Sydney. He was a camping and bushwalking enthusiast but, with four children in tow, a house provided a slightly more permanent version of tented accommodation. Moore had a great deal of respect for the land, regarding his role as essentially custodial, and the intention was to create a building that sat lightly upon it. As a result, many of the descriptions of the house liken it to a tent, a nest or even a giant seabird.

The siting of the house was immediately evident to architect and client alike, who agreed to place the building on a rock shelf, with the deck cantilevered off to the west and 'embracing an enormous Sydney red gum'. The house would command 180 degree views from its perch high on the rock. McKay's vision was for a recessive house that blended tonally with the surrounding environment but its precise execution was a more difficult matter. David Moore was one of Australia's most celebrated photographers and as such highly visual. His father was the renowned architect John D. Moore and his brother Tony Moore was also an architect. Moore himself had undertaken many architectural commissions and so understood the profession extremely well. With all those connections, Moore could have chosen anyone but, on reflection, McKay believes the Leppington Boys' Home, a project he did in conjunction with Philip Cox for the Presbyterian Church, may provide the answer.

'Moore had photographed the Leppington job and it was as much a springboard for this house as anything. It was very spare and had some innovative social thinking about it. It had an authenticity, simplicity and a modesty that David would have appreciated.'

Moore was, says McKay, 'an exacting client. My first design...he just sent me away. You always knew where you were with David,' he says philosophically. The second fared little better. 'I knew they weren't quite right myself, but the third one, he knew it was absolutely right.

'Poised on the rock, as he suggested, embracing the angophora trees, spaces flowing up and around, snug bedrooms, views from the pillow, open living spaces in and out – I think I met his asking.'

Indeed, to satisfy this list of simple, life-affirming requests, a great deal of ingenuity has been applied.

The house is essentially symmetrical, designed around a large open-plan living/dining/kitchen area, extending out to the west-facing deck. On each side of this space are small double bedrooms with views out to the bush and sky. A functional shower room sits beside each

The entrance to the house is via a timber walkway, and the door itself is protected by a canvas hood which, over time, has become as lichen-covered as the surrounding rocks. The door leads directly into the main kitchen/living/dining space and to the deck area in the treetops beyond.

bedroom. Above this area is the kids' bunk room accessed by a ladder, which in itself creates a sense of adventure.

Six bunk beds (the floor and the supports for the bed are part of the structure) fit into the space, which is open to the living area below. This ensures the children could be involved with what was happening in the main living area. Lisa Moore, David's daughter, remembers lying in bed, eavesdropping on the post-dinner conversations of the adults.

There is a communal sense about the space, achieved not only through spatial considerations, but through the spareness and simplicity of the design. As well as the clear influence of Japanese architecture, McKay also acknowledges something of the early Australian tradition in his approach. The house lacks any extraneous embellishment, giving it a sense of honesty which goes some way to explaining how it has stood the test of time. Architectural writer Philip Drew has gone so far as to call it 'a thoroughly modern masterpiece'.

Designed in 1969, the house wasn't completed until 1972, partly due to the nature of its construction. The site's beauty was matched only by its difficulty. Initially, access was by a fire trail which only extended to the base of the site. No wonder Central Coast builders shied away from such an arduous project. But, in the end, Moore found his man – Peter Velling. McKay explains, 'He was an ex-shipwright and did everything himself from beginning to end. It took him an awfully long time as he had to carry all the materials up by hand. He was very interested in the project, otherwise he

couldn't have sustained it. It was a labour of love. The only time he had assistance was to lift the truss. That was an amazing day. The posts were up, tied back to angophoras or rocks and we all hauled it up and he climbed up the truss and bolted it in place.'

Lisa Moore remembers feeling that 'we all knew that new ground was being broken, this wasn't any "ordinary" holiday house, it was an adventure.'

The house is built in tallow wood, oregon and 3/16 plywood for ceilings and walls. Its ability to sit lightly on the land comes from the precision of its design and a certain 'thinness' of execution. 'Adrian Boss, one of the finest delineators I have ever employed, did the documentation for me,' says McKay. 'Every single thing was there, every junction, every decision was made. Otherwise it simply wouldn't have fitted.' In fact, everything needed to fit because nothing is covered up. The structural workings of the building are undisguised and are the very elements that give the space its visual interest. Any patterning in this spare interior come from the lines of the beams themselves and the shafts of sunlight that filter through the slatted Japanese-style sliding doors onto the deck.

The asbestos roofing material, Super-Six AC, was chosen for its robustness and longevity, but also for aesthetic reasons. While McKay now admits it was a mistake, the hope was that it would weather and become like rock, allowing the building to recede into the landscape. And, indeed, the grey lichen-covered sheets have taken on the appearance of the surrounding bush.

As for the budget, there was never really any discussion, says McKay. 'It was a holiday house and there was nothing lavish about it. That is what I like about it. Every structural piece does two or three jobs.' In fact, the costs have been recorded as totalling $27,524.

It requires little in the way of furniture to make it feel complete. A generous dining table and benches, some portable director's chairs, low beds and fitted lights are all that is needed. Photographer Anthony Browell observed the atmosphere well. 'Despite this formal symmetry, the house seems very casual, the sort of house where discarded bathers, undies and toppled dominoes don't wreck the feel of the place.'

For Moore, the surrounding area of 'The Bay' was a source of inspiration. 'I found new meaning to life and photography in the early 1970s. The rocks and the trees, the beaches and the ocean gradually spoke to me and I learned to love them,' he said. One of his most beautiful portraits is 'The Impossible Tree', an angophora sited on the land, with a myriad twists and turns to its branches.

As it turned out, McKay was to spend more time than most architects do in houses they have designed for clients. Ian McKay married David Moore's first wife, Jenny, and so many a weekend was spent in the house with his stepchildren.

After 20 years, the inspiration Moore had taken from 'The Bay' began to wear thin and he considered selling the house. His children, in particular Lisa and Michael, were extremely keen to keep it in the family. It was a big part of their lives and they didn't want to let it go. 'The original vision is still there, it hasn't been

The entire structure of the building is exposed internally and it is this honesty and lack of embellishment that appealed to David Moore. Ian McKay points out the need for precision in design and documentation. 'Every single thing was there...every decision was made. Otherwise it simply wouldn't have fitted.' Little by way of furniture is needed. A large dining table and benches add to the spare, functional sense of the space.

OPPOSITE: The series of triangular windows running from ground level to the top of the children's sleeping area is a defining aspect of the design of the house. They form part of the intricate design of the joinery and, facing north, allow light in all day. THIS PAGE: The ladder from the ground floor leads to a mezzanine level which contains bunk beds for up to six children.

altered and I am very, very grateful for that,' says McKay. 'A good house can only come out of enjoyment and this was a wonderful experience from beginning to end. Best of all it was a venue for some very happy times, with happy people in a happy place.'

The day in the Easter holidays when my family and I visited Lisa Moore and her husband and children at the Lobster Bay House was a special one. We parked on the road and climbed the 45 degree slope to the base of the site. From there we huffed and puffed our way up the rock steps to the house itself. It has a quality that makes you feel instantly relaxed. It's to do with the lack of interior decoration, except for some weathered rubber thongs found by Moore on local beaches and nailed directly to the wood itself; the open aspect of the living areas; the climb to the bunk bed area and the direct connection to nature, all of which conspire to create the ultimate holiday house.

We had lunch, a glass of wine and walked up the stone steps (that Moore had painstakingly placed to look as though nature herself had laid them there) to Top Rock. The view did not disappoint. As we left, my son asked, 'Are those people old friends?' I explained that this was the first time we had met. McKay would, no doubt, be pleased that the house continues the spirit of 'happy times, with happy people'.

The cosy double bedrooms allow for a bed and some storage space, and the windows are placed to ensure the view is visible from the bed. Again, it is the structural elements that give form to the room, and the use of plywood for the walls and ceilings gives a sense of warmth and enclosure.

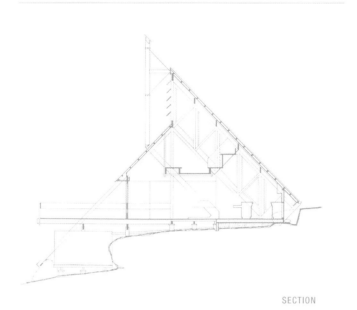

SECTION

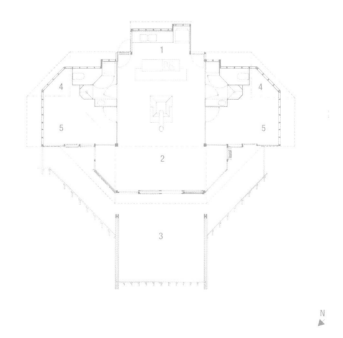

N

1. KITCHEN 2. LIVING 3. DECK 4. BATHROOM 5. BEDROOM

DETAILS THE LOBSTER BAY HOUSE

BUNK BEDS The commission was for a holiday house that could comfortably accommodate Moore's four children and, presumably, their friends. What better solution than to give them their own domain, separate from the adults but still connected? Six separate bunks could be used for reading and playing games as well as sleeping. Photographer Anthony Browell described his visit to the house as 'like walking into a giant cubby house in the trees', and for children it must have felt magical. Moore's daughter Lisa remembers the sensation of being able to 'look through the treetops to the sky, stars, storms, light and down to the water'.

STONE STEPS The landscape – the rocks and the trees – was incredibly important to Moore and a source of inspiration to him in developing his photographic work. '...my pictures became more lyrical. I did a series of female nudes which looked at the landscape of the body,' he said. Moore's aim was for the house to interfere as little as possible with the existing terrain. When he did make changes, such as building stone steps (shown above), he chose the rocks carefully and configured them in such a naturalistic way that the casual onlooker would believe them to be an existing part of the original landscape.

TIMBERS This is a house in which the honesty of the materials and the explicitness of construction are at the core of its success. While it has all the appearance of a custom-made building, it is to McKay's credit that he found a way to use standard manufactured items and shape them into a highly original design. The builder, Peter Velling, was an ex-shipwright who dedicated himself to the project and was able to deliver McKay's vision of a timber building with a certain 'thinness' of construction within a robust, dynamic overall structure. Details such as the timber sliding doors show the influence of Japanese architecture, and link back to McKay's appreciation of beauty through integrity.

LADDER Access to the bunkroom is via one of two McKay-designed ladders placed symmetrically on either side of the living area. Their construction is simple – timber treads have been fitted onto a piece of metal piping and secured underneath by a horizontal strip of metal. The treads are far apart enough to require a modicum of effort, which enhances the sense of adventure. The walls of the house are not traditionally decorated but interesting pieces of bark, washed-up rubber thongs and general flotsam and jetsam have found display space on the timber panels.

KITCHEN The kitchen is, as befits a holiday house, pleasingly basic but functional and situated just by the entrance. One suspects that after lugging bags of groceries up the hill, it is positioned exactly where it should be. It comprises two banks of cupboards – one against the rear wall and the other facing into the main living area. The kitchen is completely open to the living/dining area which, when combined with the cathedral ceiling, ensures an open, airy feel. Little in the house is closed off and this encourages the convivial holiday-house atmosphere. There are just enough points of separation and just enough opportunities for connection to keep everyone happy.

DAVID MOORE Pictured above is a portrait of the Lobster Bay House taken by David Moore. Moore (1927–2003) was one of Australia's most celebrated photographers and his images documented life in Australia for 50 years. For nine years, he collaborated with architect Philip Cox on a book, *The Australian Functional Tradition*. David Moore's work can be seen in galleries throughout Australia as well as the Musuem of Modern Art, New York, the Smithsonian Institute, Washington, and La Bibliothèque Nationale, Paris. 'I am convinced that one's mind can be freshened by balancing architectural photography with that of industry, landscape, people or the junk pile,' he said.

THERE IS NO DOUBT THAT THE MATERIAL IS INTRINSIC TO THE BUILDING'S INTENT. THE CONCRETE FEELS ORGANIC, BECOMING WEATHERED OVER TIME, WHICH LINKS IT WITH THE LANDSCAPE.

PREVIOUS PAGES: The façade is signature Iwanoff. The concrete blockwork remains original and unpainted, as Iwanoff intended. The detail shows how the blocks locked together, sometimes to form a simple design and at others to create a more complex pattern. OPPOSITE: The design of the approach to the house has a sense of gravitas. The blocks create asymmetrical columns on either side of the steps – formal and repetitive on the left and intricate and totemic on the right.

'WE WOULD TAKE THAT DESPISED OUTCAST of the building industry – the concrete block – out from underfoot in the gutter – find a hitherto unsuspected soul in it – make it live as a thing of beauty – textured as the trees.' These words were spoken by the great American architect Frank Lloyd Wright in the Twenties as he considered the structural approach he would take for client Alice Millard's second house. Wright came up with an ingenious system in which precast concrete blocks interlocked, while the surface of the blocks created pattern and textural interest on the building's façade. Fifty years later, this concept was to resonate with the work of Perth-based architect Iwan Iwanoff, who also found beauty in the concrete block. Not all the 200 or so projects he designed in his career were built from this material, but it is the work for which he is best remembered.

Iwan Iwanoff was born in Sofia, Bulgaria, in 1919 and studied architecture during the Second World War at Munich University. His artistic sensibility was expanded by the course's strong emphasis on drawing, sculpture and design, and balanced by classes in structural engineering, which honed his practical skills. In the foreword to the exhibition catalogue *The Art of Architecture – The Architectural Drawings of Iwan Iwanoff (1919–86)*, Iwanoff expert Duncan Richards points out, 'It was focused on training based upon a body of well established traditional design procedures and craft skills. The ultimate aim of the training was to develop and internalise semiautomatic "intuitive" judgments of visual order and visual coherence.' And what emerges strongly in his later work is this combination of crafted detailing within a rationalised structure. 'In my practice, the most exciting thing has always been the relationship between art and architecture,' Iwanoff said. His sketches of proposed buildings for clients were loose and lyrical with all the seductive powers of a romantic portrait. His plans, on the other hand, were intensely detailed, with every architectural element carefully delineated and described.

After working in a Munich architectural practice between 1948 and 1950 with Emil Freymuth, Iwanoff took the radical step of moving to Australia with his wife, Linda. Initially, he worked as a labourer in a local Boral factory which produced precast concete blocks until, through Bulgarian community connections, he met architect Harold Krantz. Krantz had a reputation for assisting migrant architects with the complexities of adapting to their new culture and, in many cases, hired them to work for his practice, Krantz and Sheldon. As with other migrant architects featured in this book, the Board of Architects was often reluctant to recognise qualifications gained overseas, and careers could be stunted as a result. Apart from a year with Melbourne architects Yuncken Freeman in the early Sixties, Iwanoff was employed by Krantz and Sheldon until the mid-Sixties when he was legitimately able to establish his own practice, The Studio of Iwanoff. However, right from the outset, Krantz had agreed that Iwanoff could undertake private projects, and his first independent commission was completed in 1951.

Much of Iwanoff's success came from his dedicated approach to clients and their requirements. He did not initially impose his views, instead learning as much as he could about what was wanted and how

OPPOSITE: The monochromatic door sports graphic black Perspex lozenge shapes. Sitting on the hall cabinet is a sculpture by Iwanoff's friend and fellow Bulgarian, George Kosturkov.

their lives operated. In his own words, he would 'swallow...more or less...and digest, and digest and digest...once you have all this the rest comes automatically'. The outcome would be a home that would more than satisfy his clients, and his reputation for empathy and understanding brought additional commissions. In this instance, Dr Kessell and his wife approached Iwanoff on the recommendation of a previous client, Dr Kessell's sister and her husband, Esther and David Schenberg, who owned an Iwanoff-designed house in Floreat, Perth. (The Schenbergs also commissioned a second house and a commercial building.)

Initially, the Kessells were not keen on the idea of a concrete block house but Iwanoff was able to persuade them of its appropriateness. It is a house that Iwanoff himself had earmarked as significant and it would gratify him to know that the original concrete façade is still intact. To his great disappointment, many of the exteriors of his blockwork houses were subsequently painted, which he felt 'ruined the play of light' and turned them into 'something harsh and banal'.

There is no doubt that the material is intrinsic to the building's intent. The concrete feels organic, becoming weathered over time, which links it with the landscape. The decorative element created by blockwork is subtle, in the one soft shade of grey, while the interplay of solids and voids gives it sculptural depth. When painted, the surface becomes precise and delineated, robbing the building of its quiet power.

Like Wright before him, Iwanoff sought to transform this everyday building material, with its connotations of industry and economy, into something richly textured and beautiful. In the decade since he built his own concrete block house (1965–67), his use of the material had become more elaborate and the Kessell House is a fine example of his ability to balance intricate decoration within the context of structural restraint.

His detailed plans left nothing to chance but the nature of the building work was intense. It was very different from the more conventionally constructed houses of the day, requiring specialist tradespeople who understood they were involved in the creation of something out of the ordinary. Iwanoff was known for his passion for his work, his hands-on approach and ability to infuse both clients and colleagues with enthusiasm. He told Duncan Richards the touching story of paying an unscheduled visit to a building site on a Sunday, where he found the builder proudly showing his wife and children the quality of the work he was doing there.

In the Kessell House, Iwanoff creates an intriguing sense of approach to the front door. The house is set back from the street behind a low tapering wall that follows the fall of the land. Steps from the driveway lead to a walkway and another set of steps leads to the porch, which is flanked by asymmetrical supports – one of simple square concrete block columns, the other totemic and complex. Set into a surround of glass panels in the deep porch is a boldly black-and-white patterned melamine door. Welcome to the world of Iwanoff.

The Kessell House is a large, single storey, four-bedroom family home arranged in an L-shape. To the left of the entrance is the bedroom arm, complete with a dressing room and study, both adjacent to the master bedroom. Three additional bedrooms, another bathroom, a laundry and a rumpus room at the rear (with access to the swimming pool) have all been accommodated in this section. To the right of the hallway, in the more public area, is the living room which contains a spectacular signature Iwanoff bar. Iwanoff's personality has been described as gentle, shy and friendly but his work, as this bar reveals, has all the hallmarks of exuberance, with its carved pelmet, circular lightwells and the dramatic cutaway curve of the bar itself. Professionally he was no shrinking violet.

The movement through an Iwanoff house is designed to sustain interest. Richard Black, in his article 'Eastern Block' for *Monument*, observes Iwanoff's ability to manipulate interior space. 'There is also a spatial character to the houses that is derived from the use of continuous flowing space to unify the living areas. This would be modulated by screen partitions, built-in cabinet work and sometimes through the articulation of the ceiling and floor plane. So the living areas have a permeable quality where one is always aware of adjacent spaces and activities, avoiding the feeling of separation that would have resulted from traditional walled-in rooms.'

A case in point is the sculptural timber room divider separating living and

The bar area is a tour de force of sculptural elements. The cutaway pelmet houses a fluorescent light which, through the five circular holes, illuminates the area below. The back wall of the bar has a sliding screen which opens up to access the kitchen behind.

THIS PAGE: The elaborate room divider goes some way to explaining why the cost of the interior joinery exceeded that of the building shell. Iwanoff mixed timber veneer with his favoured black Perspex for the base cabinet, and increased the functionality of the unit by housing air conditioning and audio speakers in the upper section. OPPOSITE: This close-up section shows the level of design detailing in the cabinet.

dining spaces. Another Iwanoff pièce de resistance, it is designed with a cabinet at floor level to anchor the unit and visually balance the speaker boxes that sit on either side of an integrated air conditioning unit at ceiling level. Perspex was a favoured material and the black sliding door on the cabinet provides a sleek contrast to the timber. Alongside the bar, this piece is the hero of the house in terms of dramatic impact, but throughout the less public rooms, more subtle joinery is employed. It has been recorded that the detailed interior execution cost more than the building shell itself.

As observed by architectural writer Ian Molyneaux there are 'sunscreens, stairs, balconies composed in an abstract expressionistic, sculptural manner, requiring an enormous amount of supervision by the architect'. Iwanoff's commitment to the building as a whole, inside and out, meant that the project was fairly protracted and there were many on-site revisions. In addition to specifications for built-in furniture, there was wallpaper and curtains to consider, and Iwanoff accompanied the owners to help them choose items that would enhance the overall scheme.

His commitment to his projects and perceptive approach ensured enduring relationships with his clients, often visiting them and contributing ongoing ideas for their houses. When Iwanoff joined a group of architecture students on a tour of his houses in 1983, Duncan Richards, who was present, recalls, 'What came across so strongly was the pride and pleasure of the owners in their collective efforts with the architect in creating these homes.'

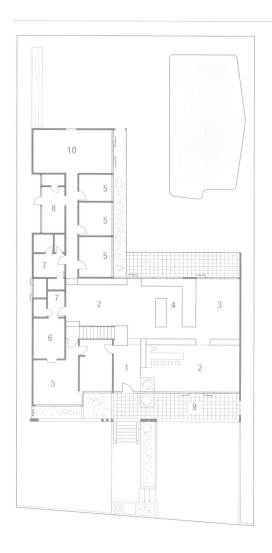

1. ENTRY 2. LIVING 3. DINING 4. KITCHEN
5. BEDROOM 6. DRESSING ROOM 7. BATHROOM
8. LAUNDRY 9. TERRACE 10. RUMPUS

N

The deep veranda, facing the street, is designed to help keep the house cool. Two Hardoy Butterfly chairs sit comfortably in the space.

CABINETRY Iwanoff's European sensibility, his love of craft and passion for sculptural form manifested itself inside his buildings as much as out. This decorative room divider is functional in as much as it separates the living and dining area, and houses shelving, an air conditioning unit and speakers. It is also highly decorative and expressionistic in its form. Tenders for the interior joinery were sought separately to the building shell and were custom-made to Iwanoff's detailed specifications. Preferred timbers were red elm and Tasmanian oak, and the design combined solid timbers with fine timber veneers used for the curved sections.

VENTILATION Unusually, the Kessell House was air conditioned at a time when few domestic residences had this luxury. In addition, Iwanoff used other cross-ventilation devices to ensure the house remained cool in the hot summer months. In the large window walls, he employed a series of Perspex panels that acted as vents at both ground and ceiling level. Originally there was a pond by the front door and the idea was that sea breezes would pass over the water and cool air would come into the house via the system of vents. The deep porch also created an area of shade.

GEORGE KOSTURKOV Sculptor George Kosturkov also came from Sofia in Bulgaria, where he studied at the Academy of Art. In 1968, as a young man of 26, he moved to Australia. Working primarily in bronze, aluminium, copper and stainless steel, he initially produced small-scale works but gradually, as his reputation grew, he undertook large-scale public and private commissions. Kosturkov was a close friend of Iwanoff and, looking at their work in parallel, it is not hard to understand a meeting of creative minds. Kosturkov's work has a natural fit within Iwanoff interiors and the owners of the Kessell House have bought five Kosturkov sculptures, three directly from the sculptor.

Dr. & Mrs. N. Kessell's Residence
Briald Place – Dianella Heights.
Architect – The Studio of Iwanoff

PRECAST CONCRETE BLOCK

Iwanoff's use of concrete blocks was highly inventive and, as Duncan Richards points out, his work illustrates an ongoing interest in 'organic expressionism'. The blocks used were all existing components created, generally, for a variety of commercial building needs and it is the ingenuity of Iwanoff's approach that makes their combinations so effective. In particular, the Kessell House utilises areas of plain block with areas of intricacy so that solidity and lightness are held in perfect balance. The blocks are a sandy limestone colour and remain unpainted as Iwanoff intended.

ARCHITECTURAL DRAWINGS In 1991,

an exhibition, *The Art of Architecture – The Architectural Drawings of Iwan Iwanoff (1919–1986),* was curated by John Nichols and Duncan Richards from the collection held by the State Archives of Western Australia. The fine arts remained an intrinsic part of Iwanoff's approach, with the exhibition illustrating his mastery of drawing skills, from the university thesis he produced on a proposed chapel in the Bulgarian mountains through to one-off domestic residences in the Perth suburbs. It is interesting that when he set up his own office in 1964, he did so under the name The Studio of Iwanoff, showing his connection to the disciplines of art and sculpture as well as architecture.

MOVING THROUGH THE HOUSE
IS TO EXPERIENCE CHANGING LIGHT
AND VARIED SPACES AS THE
VOLUMES TAPER OR OPEN UP, OR
OUTDOOR AREAS BECOME VISIBLE.

PREVIOUS PAGES: From the street, the wedge
and block construction of the timber-clad
Kenny house is evident. The exposed bracing
of the internal doors emphasises the honesty
that characterises Kenny's approach. OPPOSITE:
The entrance to the house is via a covered
pergola set well back from the main façade.

The dining table sits adjacent to the galley kitchen. The open nature of the house is visible through the doorway which leads to the office space at the front of the house. The open-tread stairs enhance this feeling of lightness.

AS A YOUNG TRAINEE ARCHITECT, JOHN KENNY was exposed to two opposing ideologies and methodologies of architectural practice. In the fourth year of his fellowship diploma course in architecture at Melbourne's RMIT, Kenny needed a work placement and, through a chance meeting hitchhiking, the opportunity arose to work part-time at Hassell and McConnell. The firm had a reputation for handling large industrial and educational projects quickly and efficiently and one of its principals, Jack McConnell, was a formidable character with establishment connections and alliances. 'McConnell was forceful, incredibly hard-working, formal and a somewhat daunting figure for an aspiring young architect,' says Kenny.

His second working environment was the office of Kevin Borland, whom Kenny met while studying at RMIT. Borland had many socio-political interests, and connections with Melbourne's left wing unions and the Communist Party. He also had a track record of avant-garde architectural solutions. His radical Rice House (1951) consisted of a series of timber arches sprayed with concrete and, along with Peter McIntyre and John and Phyllis Murphy, he was part of the design team that won the prestigious Olympic Swimming Stadium Competition in 1953. Borland had a strong sense of social responsibility, and his domestic and educational architecture reflected this. 'The office atmosphere was quite different at Kevin's with a relaxed informality. His mum would come in and make us lunch,' says Kenny. 'Kevin had seen service in World War Two and, like many of his generation, aspired to ideals and visions for a better world. He often attracted a

more independent, freer thinking type of client.' A commission that best illustrates this was Preshill, a small independent school where children were involved in setting the curriculum. Kenny was responsible for the design of the home rooms, one of the school's buildings.

Kenny worked with Borland for about three years, graduated and commenced his own practice in 1973. Soon after, he went overseas on a nine-month architectural tour that took in Scandinavia, the UK, France, the USA and Mexico. No doubt influenced by some of the preoccupations of Borland's practice, Kenny looked particularly at cluster housing in Scandinavia, the new towns of Thamesmead and Cumbernauld in England and Scotland, and the Prairie School in the States, including the houses of Frank Lloyd Wright and Burley Griffin.

Two things in particular were to impress him. The first was the work of Finnish architect and designer Alvar Aalto, whose studio he visited along with four or five of Aalto's other buildings. 'While I appreciated intellectually and admired the work of the modern movement masters like Le Corbusier, Mies van der Rohe, and Wright, and also the more contemporary architectural works of James Stirling and Louis Kahn, I felt in tune with Aalto. I liked the way in which Aalto's buildings controlled the use of forms and materials, the changing light and often the feeling of spatial movement within the interiors. To me they were fresh, functional and had a timeless quality. The Scandinavian winter is harsh, and buildings need to be designed for severe conditions. They have to work, as well as being pleasing

aesthetically internally and externally,' says Kenny.

The second influence was a group of houses, north of San Francisco, called the Sea Ranch development. Some of this coastal housing had been designed by the architect Charles Moore and his sometime partners, Lyndon, Turnbull and Whitaker, in the late Sixties and early Seventies. The style is often referred to as Bay Area Modern. 'The development had design covenants restricting the palette of materials, in addition to siting, landscaping and other environmental planning requirements.
The architects drew on the local vernacular and the houses have an appearance of random and ad hoc additions like farm buildings. They are sometimes clustered, with interlocking roof lines, clad in weathered red cedar, greyed by its seaside location,' he recalls.

When he returned to Melbourne in 1974, Kenny started up his practice again, concentrating on domestic housing, and when it came to building a house for himself and his wife, Barbara, the impact of the ideas of both Aalto and the development at Sea Ranch are evident in his design.

Finding a block to build on was not easy, and after several setbacks at auctions, a heavily pregnant Barbara trawled the inner and near-inner suburbs searching for a suitable block. She eventually came across a handwritten sign on an allotment in Kew, advertising land for sale. Its owner Edna Sharp had recently been widowed and had put a portion of her existing block up for sale. 'She knew Kevin Borland through her own political interests and involvement in the

FAR LEFT: Benchtops are of celery top pine, a timber with water resistant properties. The rangehood was designed by Kenny and custom-made for the house. The same timber was used for the ceiling lining boards and the north and south walls.
CENTRE: A desk, drawers and bookshelves are built around a horizontal window. ABOVE: A reading light is fixed to the timber-clad wall in the bedroom. In keeping with Kenny's appreciation for Scandinavian design, an Aalto stool is used as a bedside table.

Communist Party and did her homework on us before agreeing to sell,' says Kenny.

The plan for the house was based on a series of modular components, which Kenny designed specifically for this site and his family needs, but with flexibility and options in mind for other clients.

'I rationalised our spatial requirements into two basic volumes or shapes – a block and a wedge – which could be rearranged in a number of combinations and configurations depending on the site, orientation, access and outlook etc,' he says. The arrangement of the Kenny House is an offset scheme which allows for courtyards to be integrated into the plan. Other options were a linear development or even a staggered configuration where the modules were organised along a diagonal axis. Kenny hoped that his planning system, which could be realised in brick or brick veneer as well as timber, would be taken up by one of the companies specialising in project homes. With hindsight, he feels his timing was out. 'I think the whole idea of well-designed project homes was at the end of an era,' he says. 'It's a shame because the issues of sustainability, recycling and use of energy have become increasingly important. When I built this house, I wasn't even allowed to put in a water tank!'

The house is low impact. The gentle slope from north to south meant that little interference was needed to prepare the ground, and soil was redistributed rather than taken off site.

Kenny and his wife have lived in the house for more than 30 years and it is, he says in characteristically low-key fashion, 'an example of simple and rationalised residential design concerns, in its planning, assembly and use of material'.

It is not a large house by today's standards, measuring 175 m^2, but the siting, the configuration of the modules which are open to courtyards, and the manipulation of the internal volumes, create a feeling of space and light.

The house has a layered sense of approach, positioned back from the road with part of the forecourt used for off-street parking. It feels very private, set behind a low timber fence covered with ivy, and with a simply braced timber gate providing entry to the first courtyard. The front door is modest and not immediately obvious, tucked under a pergola which gives a protective feeling of semi-enclosure, and leading straight into the heart of the home – the kitchen and dining room.

The plan of the house, which has no corridors and few doors, allows for varying degrees of privacy. The modules create different zones for working, relaxing, cooking, dining, sleeping and bathing. Indeed, Kenny operated his architectural practice in the first of the block and wedge combinations facing the street.

The plan also integrates inside with out. Sited to the west of the kitchen, and north of the living area, is a generous timber-tiered courtyard which catches the northerly sun. Long slim windows, placed horizontally, allow exterior glimpses from the kitchen and the living space, and the bathroom doors slide open to another courtyard giving the sense of bathing outdoors. 'For a long time I was prone to migraines and found it soothing and a way to relax having a bath at night with the courtyard lights on and the doors open to the breeze,' says Kenny.

Moving through the house is to experience changing light and varied spaces as the volumes taper or open up, or outdoor areas become visible. 'The spaces are consistent – 2.1 metres from the floor to where the wall and ceiling meet on one side, and 2.1 metres from the floor to the underside of the mezzanine on the other,' says Kenny. Due to the absence of passages, and with very few doors, the house has a tremendous sense of flow from one space to the next. Even the open treads of the stairs enable views through to the garden.

Construction is entirely of timber. 'There was a brick by-law on the other side of the street which for some reason this side escaped,' says Kenny. Initially, he had wanted to clad the building in western red cedar but there was a significant price difference between it and the fast-growing radiata pine. Internally, Kenny opted for celery top pine, a timber that was traditionally difficult to find, but had become available due to tree felling for the controversial hydro-electric project at Lake Pedder in Tasmania. Celery top pine was being promoted in Melbourne, with a project home built in Glen Waverley to showcase the merits of native Tasmanian timbers. Kenny made enquiries; it hadn't sold well, and he had the impression they were glad to get rid of it. The celery top pine was used for all lining boards on the north and south walls and, together with the Victorian ash floor, creates a continuous band of one material. The warmth of the timber was balanced by plasterboard, painted white, on all the east and west walls. "I didn't want an entirely timber interior. The white walls keep it feeling fresh, reflect light

Kenny's architectural office was originally in the double-height block and wedge structure at the front of the house. All east and west facing walls were white painted plasterboard to reflect light and maintain a fresh Scandinavian feel.

and allow the house to be personalised with one's interests, be they books, art or craft works,' says Kenny.

The celery top pine has also been used in all the wet areas, including the shower recess. It is a tight-grained, slow-growing and very stable timber, which makes it excellent for boat-building, a hobby Kenny enjoyed in his teenage years.

'When treated with a two-pack Estapol, it endures remarkably well as long as it is maintained and end grains are not exposed,' he says. While timber benchtops are now commonplace, in the mid-Seventies Kenny was required to apply to the water authority for permission to install them.

Throughout the house, functional elements for storage and shelving have been built in, and the house furnished simply with pieces collected over the years, mixing Aalto classics with Mexican furniture and other decorative objects from the days when John and Barbara ran and operated an importing-retail business, Market Import.

'We didn't ever envisage living in the house this long, but it has worked for us, we have been happy here,' says Kenny. 'The best backhanded compliment I have ever had about it is to hear it called the Beach House. Due to its interior informality we have never had any desire to have a holiday house because we have always lived in one.'

The modular nature of the house creates courtyard areas that allow plants to be integrated into the overall scheme. The exterior cladding is radiata pine boards, fixed vertically and weathered to a pleasing grey over the years.

GROUND FLOOR   FIRST FLOOR

1. BEDROOM 2. LIVING 3. KITCHEN/DINING 4. STUDIO
5. STUDY 6. DECK 7. BALCONY 8. BATHROOM 9. STORE

N

DETAILS THE KENNY HOUSE

RANGEHOOD Kenny couldn't find a rangehood on the commercial market that suited the style of the house, so he had this one made specially for the purpose. He had used a similar design before in a client's house in Melbourne's South Yarra. The shape of the curved front is partly determined by regulations which dictate a minimum distance from the gas plate. The rangehood was made from bent plywood and then painted white. Inside the hood is a light and a fan ducted to the outside. As with many facets of the house, it combines simple aesthetic considerations with functional outcomes.

LONG WINDOWS When Kenny developed his modular plans for the house, this long slim 'slice' of a window was part of his repertoire of window and door options. It is a device he has used four times throughout the house, enabling glimpses of the outdoor spaces. Kenny feels he is of a generation that 'worked inside out, rather than outside in', and this is one of the ways in which he draws the eye outside to a view. The windows have sliding glass panes and are situated downstairs along the kitchen bench and at the rear of the living room, and upstairs in the main bedroom and studio-study.

DOORS It is a house without passages, and connecting doors are kept to a minimum. Whether they are hinged or sliding, the construction of the doors is consistent. Kenny wanted to create more interest than the conventional flat panel and decided to make a feature of the bracing and leave it exposed. Laminated treated radiata pine was the primary timber used in the door joinery. The effect is one of honesty and a certain refined vernacular rusticity.

LETTERBOX In keeping with Kenny's ability to combine the functions of a house with a clear design integrity, the letterbox also houses gas and water metering and space for the rubbish bin. Reflecting the roof line of the house, but in reverse, it is a rather endearing 'mini-me' when viewed from the street. It is also a logical place for the number of the house to be clearly visible. While it has been called a post-modern statement, Kenny sees it as a 'commonsense solution to practical concerns'.

AALTO STOOL The model 60 stool was designed in 1932 for the Viipuri Library by Alvar Aalto, the highly acclaimed Finnish architect and designer. In the 1930s, Aalto developed a technique for bending solid timber which involved making precise cuts at the point of bending. This simple three-legged stool solved the problem of additional seating plus worked perfectly as a side table. Also, the stools stack in a lovely spiral pattern and so add sculptural good looks to a room even when not in use. They are still available with tops in black or red linoleum, white or grey laminate or a natural birch veneer, produced since 1935 by Artek, Aalto's own company whose name was coined from the combination of 'Art' and 'Teknology'.

BATHROOM MIRROR Kenny used celery top pine for all wet areas, including the shower recess, and treated the wood with a two-pack Estapol finish. In the 30-plus years he has lived here, he has only sanded and recoated the wood in the bathroom three times. The hinged mirror has a recessed cupboard behind it and the design of the frame, with its rounded edges, was de rigueur for the Seventies. The original taps were laboratory ones chosen for their basic functional and industrial look. Recently they had to be replaced with very similar looking taps but with improved hydraulic performance. A rectangular laboratory sink has been set into the wooden bench.

'THE BUILDING PROCESS WAS LONG AND DRAWN OUT BECAUSE NO BUILDER WANTED TO UNDERTAKE THE PROJECT, AND SO EVERY WEEKEND POSSIBLE I WAS HELPED BY FRIENDS: AN ORTHODONTIST, THE BOAT-BUILDER AND A BIOCHEMIST.' IAN COLLINS

PREVIOUS PAGES: The Collins House as seen from Sydney's Mosman Bay. Built in an area typified by Federation red brick houses, the Collins House stands out with its clean modernist lines and fibreglass construction. The staircase, designed in steel with fibreglass treads, connects the entry level of kitchen, dining and living areas with the bedroom level below. OPPOSITE. This large picture window is a single piece of glass which was positioned with a great deal of difficulty, given the slope of the site.

THERE IS NO MISTAKING THE COLLINS HOUSE. Sited above the ferry stop in Sydney's Mosman Bay, it is a light white modernist beacon in a sea of traditional Federation terracotta and brick. From a distance it is easy to see the outline of the house's simple form and the graphic ship's hatch windows, but the material with which it is constructed is not evident until close up: the shell of the Collins House is made entirely of fibreglass.

Ian and Rosanne Collins, both architects, have lived there for more than 30 years and recall with clarity the process of finding the land, designing the house and building a home for themselves and their two daughters. 'It was Rosanne who first saw the site in 1968, and was smart enough to realise it wasn't big enough for developers to build a block of flats,' says Ian Collins. The site is small, steep and awkward, but its enviable location and outlook encouraged the Collins to buy it, realising that with two architects in the family, a building solution wouldn't be too hard to find.

'Initially we submitted a plan just to get council approval for a building on the site,' says Collins. At that stage the idea was for a brick and timber house with a degree of structural complexity. Although council passed the plan, Collins began to rethink his design and conversations with a friend, structural engineer Alex Osborne, persuaded him to move towards 'the biggest rectangle I could build on the site'. At the time the Collins purchased the land, a cream-coloured apartment block was scheduled to be built close by, and a neighbour had a modern garage, which freed Collins from any sense of obligation to conform to a Federation context.

'I was looking at the work of American architect Richard Meier and admired his use of inter-penetrating volumes. I didn't want to do a Meier-style house but he did open my eyes to new possibilities,' says Collins. Two other forces were at play – one negative and one positive. On the negative side was Collins' experience with the bricklaying trade. 'I was working in the Department of Public Works, alongside Ken Woolley and Peter Hall, and later my job was to supervise various projects. We went through a period of problems with bricks and bricklayers and I thought if I could be spared the need for that particular trade, it would be an advantage.'

At the same time, Collins' passion for sailing brought him into contact with a yacht builder who constructed Olympic-class boats. He had the capacity to mould large-scale fibreglass panels, large enough, in fact, to be used to build a house.

There were two mould shapes: a flat piece 1.5 metres wide by 3 metres high, and another forming the corner panels. The process was slow as the boat-builder, Phillip Maloney, could only produce one or two panels a week. 'We'd put them on the roof of our Ford station wagon and bring them one at a time from Lane Cove to Mosman,' recalls Rosanne. They were stacked onsite, waiting for the weekend workers to hang them in place. 'The building process was long and drawn out because no builder wanted to undertake the project, and so every weekend possible I was helped by friends: an orthodontist, the boat-builder and a biochemist,' says Collins. 'We would hook the panels in place, fixing them to the roof, as a proper curtain wall might.'

While fibreglass may be considered a lightweight material for house construction, there was nothing insubstantial about

A bank of white cabinets separates the dining area from the kitchen. The monochromatic colour scheme and bold choices of mainly Italian furniture make a confident design statement. The Seventies marble table is by Italian architect Mangiarotti and creates a sculptural centrepiece in the open-plan room.

the core structure itself. The sandstone bedrock was locked in place by rock bolts, and three thick concrete slabs were supported by sealed tubular steel columns. 'The firm of structural engineers Taylor Thomson Whitting oversaw the building and one of its principals, Dick Taylor, who had a boat moored at Mosman Bay, would call in regularly and check how we were doing.'

One of the defining features of the house are the lozenge-shaped windows which, again, reference boating. On the living level, the windows are like pairs of ship's hatches, made by inserting a shaped piece of pineboard in the standard fibreglass mould to create the window frame. 'The reason this shape is used in boats is that the seal is strongest without corners, so these windows are frameless and seal with a neoprene gasket.' The most impressive window is the wall of glass with rounded edges at the northerly end of the living area. 'I had designed it as five glass panels with fine mullions, but when the glazier saw it he said that for the same price he could provide one large piece,' says Collins Adds Rosanne: 'It took half a dozen men to carry it down the slope.'

While upstairs the view is chanced upon through pairs of windows, downstairs in the bedroom/bathroom level, it is completely embraced. 'We used a window system recommended by another sailing friend, the architect Richard Leplastrier. It's a sliding system of floor-to-ceiling glass opening up to the terrace. Richard also recommended the Vola taps in the bathrooms.' As the long side of the house faces west, it does get hot, and one of the original devices

for cooling was to pool water on the concrete roof, designed with an upstand for the purpose.

Curves recur throughout the house and the circular staircase between the levels is set in a white concave stairwell. The stair treads have been filled with fibreglass which has gained a patina over the years, giving it the appearance of tortoiseshell.

Right from the outset there was a different vision for the interior design of each level of the house. The living/dining/kitchen area was tiled in black, and the original wall treatment was of ply panels covered in black felt. 'I recall reading a book from Anthony Powell's 12-volume *A Dance to the Music of Time*. There was a description of a party in a room which was totally black, and the faces appeared to float...the idea stayed with me,' says Collins. 'The interior lining panels were pinned to the wall so that the black felt surface could soon be replaced but it stayed, and we used the panels as a pin board as well as a background for artworks.'

Downstairs was light and bright, with white ceramic floor tiles laid in the bedrooms and continuing out onto the terrace linking the two spaces. The girls' room with its white laminate cupboards and white walls was originally decorated with primary red furniture and bedspreads. 'If you look at the floorplan of the building, it doesn't read like a normal house. It is hard to tell where areas begin and leave off.' This is particularly true of the bedroom level, where the children's room was partitioned by a row of Artemide bookshelves rather than a traditional stud wall. Hence the house had the ability to evolve as family circumstances altered.

Decoratively, the interior made a strong statement – the Collins started collecting quality furniture in 1964 when they bought the Eames table and chairs for their first marital home in Greenwich. The open-plan living area, with its monochromatic palette, showcased many classic furniture pieces from the Sixties and early Seventies. These include the Anfibio sofa-bed, which was designed by Alessandro Becchi in about 1971 for the Italian company Giovanetti; the Caori coffee table, from around 1962, by Vico Magistretti; lights by Artemide and Flos, and the magnificent black marble Eros dining table, designed by an Italian architect, Angelo Mangiarotti, in about 1971.

'We have copies of *Domus* magazine from 1958,' says Rosanne. 'It was a fantastic inspiration to us.' In fact, Collins is the first to admit that the sweeping curve of the stainless steel on the kitchen benches was influenced by an article he saw in it. 'My mother had stainless steel kitchen benchtops in her cottage, so I knew the properties of the material and that it worked well, but the design inspiration came from a feature on a Mangiarotti kitchen in *Domus*,' he says.

Storage was considered right from the outset. Floor-to-ceiling cupboards run the length of the retaining wall on the lower level. 'There is even a space at one point

RIGHT: The galley kitchen combines white cabinetry with curved stainless steel benchtops. Open on both sides, with a view to the water, the kitchen is part of the main living area, but hidden from view by tall cabinets so as to not interfere with the clean lines of the overall space. FAR RIGHT: The signature windows, which recall ship's hatches, are placed in pairs along the north-west facing façade.

OPPOSITE: The view into the master bedroom. THIS PAGE: The entire bedroom floor has large sliding glass doors which open onto a generous terrace. Situated between the bedrooms are twin bathrooms, also all in white.

where you can walk through the cupboard into a "secret passage",' says Rosanne. Storage was something close to their hearts as, for many years, Rosanne ran a shop selling imported Elfa storage systems, which they have in their own home, along with modular furniture and Marimekko fabrics.

The Collins House is a one-off. While the nature of its design and materials delivered fast construction, marketing the concept was not something Collins considered. 'The fibreglass was not cheap, because it was for this use only. In addition we had some costly excavation which is normal in this area. The house probably ended up costing the same as a brick equivalent,' says Collins. Rosanne, an architect in her own right, acknowledges the house was her husband's creation. 'You see,' she explains. 'I was the client.'

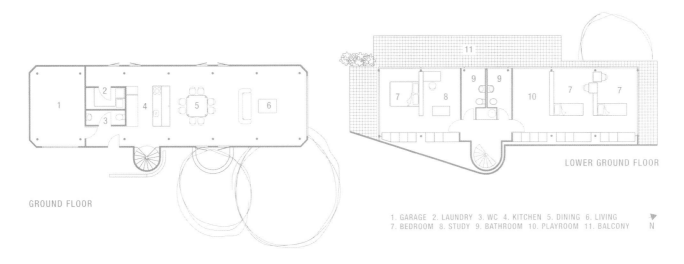

GROUND FLOOR

LOWER GROUND FLOOR

1. GARAGE 2. LAUNDRY 3. WC 4. KITCHEN 5. DINING 6. LIVING
7. BEDROOM 8. STUDY 9. BATHROOM 10. PLAYROOM 11. BALCONY   N

KITCHEN SURFACES *Domus* magazine was a tremendous source of ideas for Rosanne and Ian Collins, and in a 1974 issue they found a kitchen designed by Italian architect Angelo Mangiarotti which provided the inspiration for their kitchen. (They also had a dining table designed by Mangiarotti, so felt in tune with his aesthetic.) In the open-plan space, the kitchen forms a galley running horizontal to the dining and living areas, with a high bench used for display separating the zones. The kitchen itself is constructed in white laminate with stainless steel shaped to follow the curves of the cabinetry, creating a simple, sculptural effect. The durability of the materials has ensured that the kitchen is still in very good condition.

EXTERIOR FIBREGLASS Building a fibreglass modern home in an area of predominantly Federation houses did cause the local council some concern. While there were no domestic precedents, there was a new office building under construction in North Sydney for Sabemo, an Italian company. The façade of this building was made up of large square glass floor-to-ceiling windows set into solid sculptural frames in bright orange fibreglass. When Mosman Council asked for a sample of the material, Collins provided one from Sabemo, in bright orange... the relief of the council upon discovering it was actually to be constructed in white fibreglass probably gave the building application an increased chance of success.

COFFEE TABLE The Caori coffee table was designed by Vico Magistretti for Gavina in 1962. It is fabricated in gloss painted timber, in either black or white, and is topped with a sheet of aluminium with pull-out drawers at either end, and a 'pop-up' storage compartment in the centre for LP records or magazines. The two sides are hinged, dropping down for access to recessed storage spaces. Magistretti, who died in 2006 at the age of 85, was particularly famous for his groundbreaking work in plastics during the Sixties. The Selene (1969) and Gaudi (1970) chairs, and the Chimera light (1969), all for Artemide, were particularly celebrated.

BEDROOM The house has a light, fine sense of construction achieved by the use of fibreglass sheeting. Given that the block is small, valuable space was saved by not using brick, which would have further reduced the internal volume. The living/dining/kitchen area is at street level and the concept for the house was always to give this level a more enclosed feel with smaller windows and water glimpses, while the lower, bedroom level would be white and bright and entirely open to the view. The window system downstairs allowed for the floor-to-ceiling glass doors to open up completely to the balcony. This space was originally divided by Artemide bookshelves to create bedrooms for the Collins' two daughters. The northern window looks out onto dense greenery which provides privacy.

WINDOWS The house is characterised by the lozenge-shaped windows and doors which fall into two types of construction. The front door and the big north-facing window have frames manufactured by Plasteel. While the profiles of these frames are plastic, structural strength within the frame comes from galvanised rectangular steel tubing. This system allowed for easy fabrication of the rounded corners. The frameless glass windows use the formed recess in the fibreglass panels as framing. These windows were made of tempered glass to suit the hinges and catches available, and were fixed into the fibreglass panels before the fibreglass was lifted into position. Although one window shattered during the lifting operation, it was easily replaced.

PLASTIC SEATING This moulded plastic chair is by Svante Schoblom for Overman, a Swedish company specialising in plastic furniture based in Tranas, Sweden. The glossy plastic moulded seat is fixed to a chrome-plated sled base. The design shows a strong similarity to the Modus chair by Works Design and the Polyprop chair by Robin Day. Schoblom designed several chairs in plastic for Overman and patented designs for radical plastic flat-pack furniture in the late Seventies. The shiny black chair fits well with the monochromatic aesthetic of the Collins House. The dining table is black marble with white veining and is surrounded by Plia dining chairs in clear Perspex and chrome by Giancarlo Piretti.

BIBLIOGRAPHY

GENERAL

Archer, John, *The Great Australian Dream: The History of the Australian House*, Angus & Robertson, Sydney, 1987

Boyd, Robin, *Australia's Home*, Penguin, Melbourne, 1952

Burton Taylor, Jane, 'So Last Century', *Sydney Morning Herald*, April 13, 2006

Cuffley, Peter, *Australian Houses of the Forties and Fifties*, Five Mile Press, Melbourne, 1993

Day, Norman, *Heroic Melbourne: Architecture of the 1950s*, RMIT, Melbourne, 1995

Edquist, Harriet, 'Many Strands', *Modern in Melbourne: Melbourne Architecture 1950–75*, RMIT, Melbourne (http://users.tce.rmit.edu.au/E03159/ModMelb/mm2/lect/50_60_70/50_60.html)

Evans, Doug, 'Modernity, Progress and Place – at the Centre and at the Periphery: Melbourne Regionalism in the 1950s', *Modern in Melbourne 2*, RMIT, Melbourne (http://users.tce.rmit.edu.au/E03159/ModMelb/mm2/index.html#anchor142416)

Fromonot, Françoise, *Glenn Murcutt: Buildings and Projects*, Thames & Hudson, London, 1995

Goad, Phillip, *Melbourne Architecture*, Watermark Press, Sydney, 1999

Hayes, Babette, and Hersey, April, *Australian Style*, Paul Hamlyn, London & Sydney, 1970

'House at Rye, Victoria', *Architecture in Australia*, December 1964

Irving, Robert, *The History and Design of the Australian House*, Oxford University Press, Melbourne, 1985

Jahn, Graham, *Sydney Architecture*, Watermark Press, Sydney, 1997

Johnson, Donald Leslie, *Australian Architecture 1901–51, Sources of Modernism*, Sydney University Press, 1980

Maddex, Diane, *Fifty Favourite Houses by Frank Lloyd Wright*, Thames & Hudson, London, 2000

Tanner, Howard, *Australian Housing in the Seventies*, Ure Smith, Sydney, 1976

Taylor, Jennifer, *Australian Architecture Since 1960*, National Education Division, Royal Australian Institute of Architects

Taylor, Jennifer, *An Australian Identity: Houses For Sydney 1953–1963*, University of Sydney, Sydney, 1984

Van Schaik, Leon (ed.) *The Life Work of Guilford Bell, Architect 1912–1992*, Bookman Press, Melbourne, 1999

Watson, Anne, 'Frank Lloyd Wright', *More Space*, Issue No 7

Wilk, Christopher, *Marcel Breuer Furniture and Interiors*, Architectural Press, London, 1981

Wilson, Andrew (ed.), *Hayes & Scott: Post-War Houses*, Queensland University Press, Brisbane, 2005

HARRY SEIDLER

Glueck, Grace, 'Design Review; The Man Who Was Martha Stewart Back Before She Was', *The New York Times*, December 7, 2001

'Rose Seidler House', Historic Houses Trust brochure

Zemaitis, James, 'Russel Wright and Modern America', *Artnet*, New York

PETER MULLER

Drew, Philip, 'Profile of Peter Muller' from the Peter Muller website (www.petermuller.org)

'Peter Muller', *Architecture in Australia*, July – September 1955, p.76

Urford, J.C., 'Excerpts from Volume 1...Abstract and Introduction', *The Architecture of Peter Muller*, 1993, from the Peter Muller website (www.petermuller.org)

ROY GROUNDS

Bingham-Hall, Patrick (ed.), *A Short History of Melbourne Architecture*, Pesaro Publishing, Sydney, 2002

Ghezzi, Sebastiano, 'Roy Grounds: Bibliographical Details', *Modern in Melbourne*, RMIT, Melbourne (http://users.tce.rmit.edu.au/e03159/ModMelb/mm2/modmelbprac2/rg/groundsbio.htm)

Hamann, Conrad, *Modern Architecture in Melbourne: the Architecture of Grounds Romberg and Boyd, 1927–1971*, Monash University, Melbourne, 1979

Miles, Martin, 'Roy Grounds', *Canberra House* (www.canberrahouse.com)

Miles, Martin, 'The Post-War Melbourne Regional Style', *Canberra House* (www.canberrahouse.com)

'Roy Grounds House and Flats', *National Trust* (www.nationaltrust.org.au/pdfs/ntvic1.pdf)

'Sir Roy (Burman) Grounds', *ArchINFORM* (www.archinform.net)

Tanner, Howard (ed.), *Architects of Australia*, Macmillan, Melbourne and New York, 1981

PETER MCINTYRE

Kiely, Annemarie, 'Take the A-Frame', *Belle*, August/September 2001

'Modern in Melbourne 2: Melbourne Architecture 1950–75: Practice Archives: Peter McIntyre: McIntyre Residence 1955', RAIA, Melbourne (http://users.tce.rmit.edu.au/E03159/ModMelb/mm2/index.html#anchor142416)

RUSSELL JACK

Dunphy, Milo, 'Growth of an Australian Architecture', *Hemisphere Magazine*, August 1962

Keens, Leta, 'Wall and Peace', *Belle*, August/September 2001

O'Brien, Geraldine, 'Houses that Russell, John and Keith Built', *Sydney Morning Herald*, April 25, 2003

ROBIN BOYD

National Trust of Australia (Victoria) 'National Trust Launches Boyd Foundation' (www.nattrust.com.au)

Searle, Geoffrey, *Robin Boyd: A Life*, Melbourne University Press, Melbourne, 1995

MCGLASHAN AND EVERIST

Goad, Philip, and Trimble, Judith, *Living in the Landscape: Heide and Houses by McGlashan and Everist*, exhibition catalogue

Houston, Melinda, 'Get Inside the Art of Heide', *The Age*, July 19, 2006

Jolley, E., Colton, C., Ong, V., Chan, S.S., 'David McGlashan (McGlashan & Everist)', Modern in Melbourne, RMIT, Melbourne (http://users.tce.rmit.edu.au/E03159/ModMelb/mm2/modmelbprac2/dm/dmbio.htm)

ENRICO TAGLIETTI

Favaro, Paola, 'Interviews with the Canberra Architect Enrico Taglietti (At the Architect's Office in Manuka on 23 April 2003 and 8 October 2003)', *Architectural Theory Review 10*, number 2, 2005, University of Sydney, Sydney

Metcalf, Andrew, *Canberra Architecture*, Watermark Press, Sydney, 2003

Miles, Martin, '61 Sullivan Crescent, Wanniassa (1980)', *Canberra House* (www.canberrahouse.com)

Miles, Martin, 'Enrico Taglietti Image Gallery', *Canberra House* (www.canberrahouse.com)

Tadi, Ettore, *Enrico Taglietti: Architect In Australia*, Lodigraf, Milan, 1979

'Taglietti's Unique Sculptural, "Organic" Style', *The Real Estate Times*, September 26, 1998
Whitelaw, Ann, 'Exotic Roofs, Three Levels, and Hilltop Views', *The Canberra Times*, July 2, 1968

NEVILLE GRUZMAN
Bevan, Robert, 'Stage Craft', *Monument,* No 73
Goad, Phillip, *Gruzman: An Architect and His City*, Craftsman House, Victoria, 2006
Haskell, John, 'Towards an Australian Idiom: the Architecture of Neville Gruzman', *Art & Australia*, Volume 23, Number 2, Summer 1985, pp. 231–236
Mayoral Minutes, Woollahra Municipal Council, 'Tribute to the Life and Work of the Late Neville Gruzman, AM', May 9, 2005
Rickard, Bruce, and Goad, Phillip, 'Radar Obituary: Vale Neville Gruzman', *Architecture Australia*, July/August 2005
Swann, Graham, 'The Work of Neville Gruzman: Hills House, Turramurra, 1960 to 1983', *The Twentieth Century Heritage Society of NSW* (http://www.twentieth.org.au/People/Gruzman/Hills/Hills.html)
Weirick, James, 'Harry Howard: Landscape Architect, 1930–2000', *Sydney Morning Herald*, October 7, 2000

BRUCE RICKARD
Barouch, Judy, 'Mirrabooka – A Real Thriller', The National Trust Website (www.nsw.nationaltrust.org.au)
Royal Australian Institute of Architects, 'RAIA Tour of Houses Designed by Bruce Rickard' brochure, 18 August 2002. Contains excerpt from *Contemporary Architects* by Muriel Emanuel, 1994

HUGH BUHRICH
Farrelly, Elizabeth, 'A Dreamhouse You'd Actually Live In', *Sydney Morning Herald*, June 22, 2004
Farrelly, Elizabeth, 'Hugh Buhrich's House' *Architecture Australia*, July/August 2004
Myers, P., Lassen, C., Durbach, N., 'Obituary: Vale Hugh Buhrich' *Architecture Australia*, September/October 2004

IAN MCKAY
Davies, Alan, *David Moore: 100 Photographs*, exhibition catalogue, State Library of NSW, Sydney, 2005

Drew, Philip, 'Radar Delight', *Architecture Australia*, July/August 2002
Reinmuth, Gerard (compiled by), 'Central Coast Houses Then and Now', *Architectural Review (AR)*, Number 64, Winter 1998
Woolard, Steve, *Ian McKay 1961–1992: The Sydney School: Thirty Years of Development*, thesis, University of Queensland, Brisbane, 1992

IWAN IWANOFF
Black, Richard, 'Eastern Block', *Monument*, No 73
'Documentation of Places for Entry in the Register of Heritage Places' (Kessell House, Data Base Number 06658) Register of Heritage Places, May 2004
Lloyd Wright, Frank, *An Autobiography*, Pomegranate Communications, 2005
Neille, Stephen, 'West Coast Cool', *Monument*, No 69
Nichols, John and Richards, Duncan, *The Art of Architecture: The Architectural Drawings of Iwan Iwanoff (1919–1986): An Exhibition of Architectural Drawings by the Architect Iwan Iwanoff From the Collection held by the State Archives of Western Australia* (April 15 to May 13, 1991) Alexander Library Building, Perth Cultural Centre, Perth, 1991
Richards, Duncan, 'A Temple for Suburban Living: The Iwanoff House, Lifford Road, Floreat Park, Western Australia (1965–1967)', *Transition 44/45*, RMIT, Melbourne, 1994

IAN COLLINS
Walter, Betsy, 'Innovation and Open Plans', *Belle*, September/October 1978

CONVERSION GUIDE
1 hectare = 2.47 acres
1 millimetre = 0.039 inches
1 centimetre = 0.39 inches
1 metre = 39 inches
1 m^2 = 10.76 square feet
1 kilometre = 0.62 miles
1 kilogram = 2.2 pounds

Note: It took a number of years from first sketch stage to completion for most of the houses in this book. The year indicated on opening pages refers to the date of completion.

INDEX

ACKNOWLEDGEMENTS

The aim of this book is to capture what is still intact, in 2007, of the work of architects practising in Australia in the Fifties, Sixties and Seventies. The challenge was to find houses that were as close as possible to the architects' original intent – houses that weren't heavily renovated, and the interior furnishings of which were stylistically sympathetic, if not original. The final selection of 15 is by no means definitive. There are many architects whose houses I would love to have included but, unfortunately, lack of permission to photograph and other constraints made it impossible.

When I was commissioned to write the book, I knew of five such houses. Finding the other ten was a source of frustration and genuine delight and I remain grateful to the people who helped me in the task of sourcing them.

Thanks to: Scott Robertson, Douglas Evans and the members of Docomomo Australia, Anne Higham at the RAIA, Dean Angelucci, Graham Fisher, Donald Campbell, Caroline Quaine, Annemarie Kiely, and Tim Reeves.

Enormous thanks to Michael Wee for his wonderful photographs, and Andrea Healy for her art direction and for creating a book design that does the photographs justice. Thanks to Leta Keens whose editing skills and knowledge of the period I have benefited greatly from. Thanks to Georgia Fox for her ability to source obscure articles, in obscure journals, and to Jason Grant for his generosity with his time helping on photographic shoots.

My heartfelt thanks to my husband, David Harrison, whose tremendous knowledge of twentieth century furniture, endless patience and sound advice have made the whole book possible.

I am grateful to the homeowners who permitted us to photograph their houses – Kate McCann at the Audette House; Martin Hiscock at the Grounds House; Kerrie and Michael Hills at the Rosenburg/Hills House; Neil Buhrich at the Buhrich House II; Lisa Moore at the Lobster Bay House; Philip Goldacre and Suzanne Northcotte at the Dingle House; Matthew and Merja Shield at the Kessell House.

Thanks to the architects for their time – Peter Muller; Peter McIntyre; Russell Jack; Enrico Taglietti; John Kenny; Bruce Rickard; Ian McKay; Ian and Rosanne Collins; Neil Everist; Stan Symonds; Bruce Robertson.

Thanks to Penleigh Boyd, Mrs Patricia Davis, Tony Lee and Jennifer Aughterson, Andrew Wilson, Andrew Mitchell, Hans and Pam Snelleman, Margaret Tuckson, Margot Gruzman, Penelope Seidler, Andre Fombertaux, Jane Johnson, Bin Dixon-Ward, Sandra Gray, Don Fulton, Eve McGlashan and Tasker Ryrie.

And finally, thanks to Kay Scarlett for recognising the potential for this book and to Diana Hill for shepherding it through the occasionally fraught process.

First published in 2007 by Murdoch Books, an imprint of Allen & Unwin
This revised edition published in 2014 by Murdoch Books, an imprint of Allen & Unwin.

Murdoch Books Australia
83 Alexander Street
Crows Nest NSW 2065
Phone: +61 (0)2 8425 0100
Fax: +61 (0)2 9906 2218
www.murdochbooks.com.au

Murdoch Books UK
Erico House, 6th Floor.
93-99 Upper Richmond Road
Putney, London SW15 2TG
Phone: +44 (0) 20 8785 5995
Fax: +44 (0) 20 8785 5985

Concept and Design: Andrea Healy
Photography: Michael Wee, unless specified
Editor: Leta Keens

Credits:
Page 9 photographed by David Moore, courtesy of the architect. © the estate of David Moore.
Page 10 (left) photographed by Max Dupain; (right) from Hayes and Scott archive, UQFL278, Box 1,
    held at the Fryer Library, University of Queensland.
Page 11 courtesy of Neil Clerehan.
Page 14 photographed by David Moore, courtesy of the architect. © the estate of David Moore.
    Drawing by Ken Woolley.
Page 15 photographed by architect Jean Fombertaux, courtesy of Andre Fombertaux.
Page 16 photographed by David Moore, courtesy of the architect. © the estate of David Moore.
Page 17 courtesy of Stan Symonds.
Page 18 photographed by Mark Strizic, courtesy of Bell Fisher Architects.
Page 19 photographed by Max Dupain, courtesy of Glenn Murcutt.
Page 45 photograph of model courtesy of Peter Muller.
Page 98 drawing by Penleigh Boyd, The Robin Boyd Foundation.
Page 185 Ian McKay's Lobster Bay House photographed by David Moore, courtesy of the architect.
    © the estate of David Moore.
Page 199 Iwan Iwanoff drawing courtesy of Battye Library 4400A/272/8
Redrawn plans by Robert Parkinson (pages 30, 68, 112, 136, 168, 196, 223)

A cataloguing-in-publication entry is available from the catalogue of the
National Library of Australia at www.nla.gov.au.

A catalogue record for this book is available from the British Library.

Colour reproduction by Splitting Image, Clayton, Victoria.

Printed by 1010 Printing International Ltd.

Reprinted 2014

COVER PHOTO: The living area of the Buhrich House, with its wave ceiling and hand-crafted furnishings, backs onto bushland and faces a spectacular view of the water.
FRONT ENDPAPER: The view through the angophoras to Brisbane Water from Ian McKay's Lobster Bay House. PAGE 2: The entrance to Robin Boyd's house is via an open-tread wooden staircase sited under a protective canvas awning. PAGE 4: A cantilevered cabinet in a bedroom of Hugh Buhrich's house in Sydney's Castlecrag.
BACK ENDPAPER: The view at dusk of the Spit Bridge, Sydney, from Bruce Rickard's Marshall House.